Official Guide to the
Wales Coast Path: South Wales Coast

Swansea to Chepstow

Limestone cliffs on the Glamorgan Heritage Coast

Official Guide to the Wales Coast Path
South Wales Coast

River Tawe at Swansea to River Wye at Chepstow

115 miles / 185 kilometres of superb coastal walking

Dennis & Jan Kelsall

Northern Eye
www.northerneyebooks.co.uk

Northern Eye

First published 2017
This revised and updated edition 2024

Northern Eye Books Ltd
Northern Eye Books, Tattenhall,
Cheshire CH3 9PX

Text: Dennis & Jan Kelsall
Series editor: Tony Bowerman
Introductory section: Tony Bowerman

Design: Carl Rogers
Photographs: Dennis & Jan Kelsall, Tony Bowerman, © Crown copyright (2023) Visit Wales, Joan Gravell /Alamy Stock Photo, Shutterstock, Dreamstime

© Northern Eye Books Limited 2024

Dennis & Jan Kelsall have asserted their rights under the Copyright, Designs and Patents Act, 1988 to be identified as the authors of this work. All rights reserved.

This book contains mapping data licensed from the Ordnance Survey with the permission of the Controller of Her Majesty's Stationery Office. All maps based on the 1:50,000 Landranger map.

© Crown copyright 2024. All rights reserved.
Licence number 100047867

ISBN **978-1-914589-04-1**

A CIP catalogue record for this book is available from the British Library

www.northerneyebooks.co.uk
www.walescoastpath.co.uk

Email: tony@northerneyebooks.co.uk

For trade and sales enquiries, please call:
01928 723 744

Important Advice: The route described in this book is undertaken at the reader's own risk. Walkers should take into account their level of fitness, wear suitable footwear and clothing, and carry food and water. It is also advisable to take the relevant OS maps with you in case you get lost and leave the area covered by our maps.

Whilst every care has been taken to ensure the accuracy of the route directions, the publishers cannot accept responsibility for errors or omissions, or for changes in the details given. Nor can the publisher and copyright owners accept responsibility for any consequences arising from the use of this book.

If you find any inaccuracies in either the text or maps, please write or email us. Thank you.

Acknowledgements: Warm thanks are due to everyone who helped make this book a reality. Thank you, in particular, to Natural Resources Wales' officer Quentin Grimley for his friendly advice and support. Thanks to Andrew Mason & Alison Roberts — Bridgend, Chris Dale — Swansea; Lee Barrett & Catrin Evans — Neath Port Talbot; Alison Roberts — Bridgend; Gwyn Teague — Vale of Glamorgan; Jenn Griffiths & Tricia Cottnam — Cardiff; Luke Stacey & Andy Briscombe — Newport; Ruth Rourke & Matthew Lewis — Monmouthshire; Ben Tasker — National Trust; Alex Edwards — Porthkerry Country Park. Thanks, too, to the many tourism officers, museum and library staff, Wales on View picture researchers, freelance photographers, and everyone else who has played their part. And, finally, thanks to Peter Bray for his passionate quote explaining why the Wales Coast Path is so special

www.northerneyebooks.co.uk
www.walescoastpath.co.uk

 @WalesCoasUK
@Northerneyeboo

 @wales_coast_path

Contents

Wales Coast Path: Discover the shape of a nation 6
  Wales Coast Path: An 870-mile coastal adventure 8
  The Best of the South Wales Coast 28
  South Wales Coast: Part of the Wales Coast Path 30
    Walking the South Wales Coast — map and distance chart 34
  Day Sections 35
  Limited for time? The South Wales Coast in a nutshell 42
  A brief history of the South Wales Coast 44
  Wildlife along the South Wales Coast 50
  Heritage coast, sand dunes and reclaimed nature reserves 52

The South Wales Coast section of the Wales Coast Path
  Day Section 1: Swansea (River Tawe) to Port Talbot 60
    Aberavon 72
    Cwm Afan 76
  Day Section 2: Port Talbot to Porthcawl 78
    Port Talbot steel industry 86
    Kenfig National Nature Reserve 90
  Day Section 3: Porthcawl to Ogmore 98
  Day Section 4: Ogmore to Llantwit Major 108
    Glamorgan Heritage Coast 112
    Nash Point lighthouses 120
  Day Section 5: Llantwit Major to Barry Island 124
  Day Section 6: Barry Island to Cardiff Barrage 140
    Barry Docks 146
  Day Section 7: Cardiff Barrage to Newport (Transporter Bridge) 158
    Cardiff Bay 160
    Welsh coal 164
  Day Section 8: Newport (Transporter Bridge) to Redwick 176
    Newport Wetlands RSPB Reserve 182
  Day Section 9: Redwick to Chepstow 190
  Useful Information 202
  Wales Coast Path: Official Guides 206

Official Guides to the Wales Coast Path
The Official Guides to the Wales Coast Path are endorsed by **Natural Resources Wales,** the body responsible for coordinating the development of the route. The guides split the Path into seven main sections with a guide for each. Together, they cover the entire 870-mile Path from the outskirts of Chester in the north to Chepstow in the south.

For details of the full range of Official Guides to the Wales Coast Path, see:
www.walescoastpath.gov.uk/plan-your-trip/guidebooks/

Wales Coast Path
Discover the shape of a nation

WALES IS THE LARGEST COUNTRY IN THE WORLD with a continuous path around its entire coast. The **Wales Coast Path** promises 870 miles/1400 kilometres of unbroken coastal walking, from the outskirts of Chester in the north to Chepstow in the south. Along the way you'll experience the very best of Wales: stunning scenery, stirring history, Welsh culture, and wildlife in abundance. If you tackle only one big walk in your life, make it this one. It's unmissable.

Conwy Castle, Conwy

St Cwyfan's church, Anglesey

Chough

Ty Coch Inn, Llŷn Peninsula

Harlech Castle, Gwynedd

Ynyslas NNR, Ceredigion

Porthgain harbour, Pembrokeshire

Puffin

Rhossili Bay, Gower

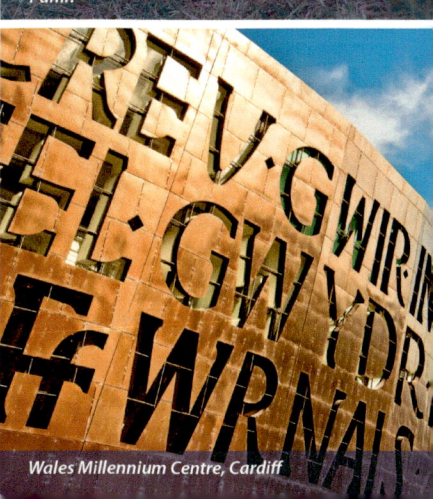
Wales Millennium Centre, Cardiff

Wales Coast Path
An 870-mile coastal adventure

When the **Wales Coast Path** opened in May 2012, Wales became the largest country in the world with a continuous path around its entire coast. Walkers can now enjoy unparalleled coastal walking around the Welsh seaboard from top to bottom: from the outskirts of the ancient walled city of Chester, on the Dee estuary in the north, to the pretty market town of Chepstow, on the Severn Estuary, in the south.

The official, signposted and waymarked path covers roughly 870 miles/1400 kilometres and starts and finishes close to the ends of the historic 180 mile/285 kilometre Offa's Dyke National Trail. This means keen walkers can make a complete circumnavigation of Wales; a total distance of around 1,050 miles/1,690 kilometres. Ever keen for a new challenge, a few hardy walkers had already completed the full circuit within months of the Wales Coast Path's opening.

Nash Point, Glamorgan Heritage Coast

But whether you choose to walk the whole Path in one go, in occasional sections, or a few miles at a time, you're in for a real treat. There's something new around every corner, and you'll discover places that can only be reached on foot. Visually stunning and rich in both history and wildlife, the path promises ever-changing views, soaring cliffs and spacious beaches, sea caves and arches, wildflowers, seabirds, seals and dolphins, as well as castles, cromlechs, coves and coastal pubs. It's a genuinely special landscape.

This visual and ecological richness is recognised nationally and internationally. In fact, the Wales Coast Path runs through 1 Marine Nature Reserve, 1 Geopark, 2 National Parks, 3 Areas of Outstanding Natural Beauty, 3 World Heritage Sites, 7 official and unofficial nudist beaches, 11 National Nature Reserves, 14 Heritage Coasts, 17 Special Protection Areas, 21 Special Areas of Conservation, 23 Historic Landscapes, 42 Blue Flag beaches, and 111 marine Sites of Special Scientific Interest. Large stretches of coast are also managed and protected by Wildlife Trusts, the RSPB and the National Trust.

Long-distance walkers will enjoy the unbroken path, the solitude, the coast's constantly changing moods and the back-to-nature challenge. Holiday and weekend walkers can recharge their batteries, see something new, and regain a necessary sense of perspective. Families can potter, play and explore. And locals can walk the dog, jog, get fit and rediscover their home patch. Whatever your preferences, the Wales Coast Path promises something for everyone.

"I just loved (nearly) every minute of this epic walk. A truly remarkable journey ..."

Peter Bray — the first over-75 year old to walk the Wales Coast Path

All or Part?

So, what's the best way to walk the Wales Coast Path? The 870 mile/1400 kilometre route covers the whole of the Welsh seaboard and is the longest and probably the best of all Britain's long-distance challenges.

But of course, not everyone has the time, energy or inclination to walk it all at once. Instead, most people start with a short stretch, discover they love it, and come back for more.

Section by section
1. North Wales Coast
2. Isle of Anglesey
3. Llŷn Peninsula
4. Snowdonia & Ceredigion Coast
5. Pembrokeshire Coast Path
6. Carmarthen Bay & Gower
7. South Wales Coast

Wales Coast Path 11

1. North Wales Coast
Chester to Bangor
80 miles/125 kilometres
7 Day Sections

Undulating coast. Vast Dee estuary, traditional seaside towns, limestone headland, and Conwy mountain

2. Isle of Anglesey
Circuit of island from Menai Bridge
125 miles/200 kilometres
12 Day Sections

Grand coastal scenery from tidal straits to bays, estuaries, dunes and cliffs. Area of Outstanding Natural Beauty

3. Llŷn Peninsula
Bangor to Porthmadog
110 miles/180 kilometres
9 Day Sections

Unspoilt peninsula with bays, coves and cliffs, tipped by Bardsey Island. Area of Outstanding Natural Beauty

4. Snowdonia & Ceredigion Coast
Porthmadog to Cardigan
140 miles/225 kilometres
12 Day Sections

Low-lying dunes and big estuaries followed by steeper, grassy sea cliffs with dramatic coves and bays

5. Pembrokeshire Coast Path
Cardigan to Tenby/Amroth
185 miles/300 kilometres
14 Day Sections

Varied, beautiful, popular. The Pembrokeshire Coastal Path is a National Trail and coastal National Park

6. Carmarthen Bay & Gower
Tenby to Swansea
130 miles/208 kilometres
12 Day Sections

Long sandy beaches, tidal estuaries, dramatic rocky coast. Area of Outstanding Natural Beauty

7. South Wales Coast
Swansea to Chepstow
115 miles/185 kilometres
9 Day Sections

Traditional beach resorts, seafaring and industrial landscapes. Heritage Coast, National Nature Reserves

Pier group: *Llandudno Pier and the Great Orme, North Wales coast*

Wales: Top to bottom

Walking the whole 870 miles/1400 kilometres of the Wales Coast Path in one go is an increasingly popular challenge. Some people have even run all the way. By a curious coincidence, the overall distance is almost exactly the same as Britain's famous top-to-bottom route, from John o' Groats to Land's End — a very long way.

The Wales Coast Path will take you from the outskirts of Chester down the broad Dee estuary, along the North Wales coast with its traditional seaside resorts and impressive limestone headlands at Little and Great Orme, past Conwy Castle, over Conwy Mountain and on along the wooded Menai Straits. The Path then loops around the rugged, offshore Isle of Anglesey, or Ynys Môn, passes the walled town of Caernarfon and its castle before heading around the remote Llŷn Peninsula with Bardsey Island balanced at its tip. From Criccieth and Porthmadog the Path pushes south past Harlech castle — kissing the western rim of the Snowdonia National Park — and on down the majestic sweep of Cardigan Bay with its beautiful, open estuaries. It then rounds Pembrokeshire — Britain's only coastal National Park — with its

sparkling bays and lofty cliffs. Striding through Carmarthenshire and crossing the wide Towy and Tâf estuaries, the Path curves around the lovely Gower Peninsula into Swansea Bay. Beyond the striking Glamorgan Heritage Coast, the Path runs along the Cardiff Bay waterfront to Cardiff, the lively capital of Wales. From there, it's only a short stretch alongside the broad Severn estuary to the pretty market town of Chepstow on the Welsh-English border and the southern end of the Wales Coast Path.

Only the fittest, most determined walkers can hope to complete the entire Path in 6-7 weeks, averaging 20 or so miles a day.

At a more leisurely pace — allowing time to soak up the atmosphere and enjoy the views, and with regular pauses to watch the wildlife, swim, enjoy a quiet drink or visit some of the fascinating places along the way — you should allow around 3 months for the whole trip.

Remember, though, the Wales Coast Path is a challenging route with plenty of rough ground, narrow paths and ups-and-downs (an overall total ascent and descent of 95,800 feet/ 29,200 metres). There are tempting detours and places to see along the way, too. So it's perhaps best to plan slightly shorter and more realistic daily distances than you might ordinarily cover.

You should also allow extra time for the unexpected, to rest or to hole up in bad weather. As a rule of thumb, it's better to be ahead of schedule, with time to enjoy the experience, rather than always having to push ahead to reach the next overnight stop.

The Official Guidebooks in this series break the path down into seven main sections (see the map on page 10), each of which is then sub-divided into carefully-planned 'Day Sections' — usually averaging around 10-15 miles each. These typically start and finish either in, or near easy-to-reach towns, villages or settlements, many of them on bus routes, and with shops, pubs, restaurants, cafés and places to stay nearby.

No matter how long it takes, walking the whole of the Wales Coast Path is a real achievement. For most of us, it would be the walk of a lifetime.

Walking around Wales a bit at a time

Yet, understandably, most people don't want to walk the whole path in one go. Instead, they prefer to do it bit by bit, often over several years: during annual and bank holidays, over long weekends, or as the whim takes them. Done in this leisurely fashion, the walk becomes a project to ponder, plan, and take pleasure in.

A popular way to enjoy the path is to book a short holiday close to a section of the path, and do a series of day walks along the surrounding coast, returning to your base each night.

The Menai Strait separates the Isle of Anglesey from mainland Snowdonia

Arch angels: *Exploring the dramatic Bwa Gwyn sea arch on the west coast of Anglesey*

Some people like to catch a train (especially along the North Wales Coast), bus or taxi to the start of their day's walk and then walk back (see the information at the start of each day section).

Another approach is to drive to the end of your planned section and then get a pre-booked local taxi to take you back to the start; this costs only a few pounds and lets you walk in one direction at your own pace.

If you're planning to walk a section over several days before returning to your starting point by bus or train, call Traveline on 0870 6082608 or visit **www.traveline-cymru.org.uk** for help with timetables and itineraries.

Best time to go?

Britain's main walking season runs from Easter to the end of September. Although the Wales Coast Path is delightful throughout the year, the best walking weather tends to be in late spring as well as early and late summer.

Although the Easter holiday is busy, spring is otherwise a quiet time of year. The days are lengthening and the weather getting steadily warmer. Migrant birds and basking sharks are returning to Wales from farther south. The weather is also likely to be dry.

Early summer is ideal for walking. May and June enjoy the greatest number

Sacred Isle?: *Looking across the Sound to Bardsey Island, or Ynys Enlli, at the tip of Llŷn*

of sunshine hours per day (the average for May is 225 hours, and for June 210 hours) and the lowest rainfall of the year (average for May is 50mm, June is 51mm). You'll also have the accompaniment of a spectacular array of spring flowers and the chance to see breeding sea birds at their best.

High summer is the busiest season, particularly during the school holidays in July and August. Both the beaches and the Coast Path are likely to be packed in places. Finding somewhere to stay at short notice can be tricky, too — so it's best to book well in advance. However, the long sunny days are certainly attractive, and you can often walk in shorts and a T-shirt.

By September most visitors have returned home, and you'll have the Coast Path largely to yourself. The weather remains good and the sea is still warm enough for swimming. Sunny days often stretch into September, with the first of the winter storms arriving in late September and October. Autumn also means the coastal trees and bracken are slowly turning from green to red, orange and gold.

Winter brings shorter, colder days with less sunlight and other disadvantages: unpredictable weather, stormy seas, high winds and even gales

along with closed cafés and accommodation. But for experienced walkers, the cooler days can bring peace and solitude and a heightened sense of adventure.

Welsh weather

Like the rest of Britain, Wales is warmed by the Gulf Stream's ocean current and enjoys a temperate climate. This is particularly true of the country's west coast. Because Wales lies in the west of Britain, the weather is generally mild but damp. Low pressure fronts typically come in off the Irish Sea from the west and southwest, hitting the coast first and then moving inland to the east. This means rain and wet weather can occur at any time of year, so you should always take good waterproofs and spare clothes with you.

For more weather or a five-day forecast, visit **www.metoffice.gov.uk** or **www.bbc.co.uk/weather**. Several premium-rate national 'Weatherlines' give up-to-date forecasts, and the Snowdonia and Pembrokeshire National Parks websites provide local information, too.

Which direction?

The Official Guide books give directions from north to south, starting in Chester and ending in Chepstow. This means walkers will enjoy the sun on their faces for much of the way. Most luggage transfer services also run in this direction. Nonetheless, the path can be tackled in either direction. It's just easier to go with the flow.

Which section?

Choosing which part of the Wales Coast Path to walk depends in part on where you live, how long you've got, and the kind of scenery you prefer.

Sections vary considerably. Arry Beresford-Webb, the first person to run the entire Path in 2012 said, 'I was stunned by the diversity of the Path. Each section felt like I was going through a different country.'

Some stretches are fairly wild, while others are more developed. Parts of the Isle of Anglesey, Llŷn Peninsula, Cardigan Bay and Pembrokeshire are often remote and away from large settlements. Other stretches, such as North Wales or the South Wales coast around Swansea, Cardiff and Newport are busier, and often close to popular seaside towns or industry.

The terrain varies too. Much of the North Wales coast is low-lying but punctuated with occasional headlands; as are much of Cardigan Bay, Carmarthen Bay, and parts of the Glamorgan Heritage Coast.

Portmeirion village seen across the sandy mouth of Afon Dwyryd

In contrast, the Isle of Anglesey, Llŷn Peninsula, Pembrokeshire and Gower are often rocky with high sea cliffs, dramatic headlands, offshore islands and intimate coves.

Self sufficient or supported?

The other key decision for walkers is whether to arrange everything yourself or let experts do it for you. For many people, devising their own itinerary and working out how to travel and where to stay is part of the fun. Others prefer to let one of the specialist walking holiday companies create the itinerary, book accommodation, arrange luggage transfers, meals, and side trips. The main companies are listed at the back of the book.

Accommodation

There are plenty of places to stay within easy reach of the Wales Coast Path all around Wales. Most walkers either camp or stay in bed and breakfast accommodation; usually a mix of the two. There are plenty of hostels and bunkhouses along the way but, unfortunately, they are too unevenly spaced to provide accommodation every night.

Accommodation may be fully booked during peak holiday seasons, so it's advisable to book well ahead. Local Tourist Information Centres (TICs) will often know all the local accommodation providers, know who has vacancies, and can help with booking. **For online booking visit: www.walescoastpath.co.uk.** This website has a specific section for planning your walk, which includes booking a range of accommodation options at the end of each **Day Section** (see page 204).

Backpacking

Backpacking adds an extra dimension to the walking experience: being outdoors for days at a time, watching the sunrise and sunset, gazing at the stars overhead without artificial light getting in the way. But don't underestimate how much a heavy pack can slow you down. The secret is to travel as light as possible; the lightest tent or bivvi bag, a lightweight sleeping bag and waterproofs, and a single change of clothes.

There are plenty of official campsites along the busier sections of the Wales Coast Path. However, many are on small farms and may not advertise. Elsewhere campsites are often few and far between, and may need searching for. During peak season some may also be full, so it's advisable to book ahead. But remember, most sites are closed during the winter (typically from November to Easter, and often longer).

Coastal chat: *Walkers meeting on the coast path above Ceibwr Bay, in Pembrokeshire*

Unofficial 'wild camping' is a grey area. There is no legal right in England or Wales to 'wild camp' anywhere, including alongside the path. Every scrap of land in Britain belongs to someone, and many landowners frown on campers. So it makes sense to ask before pitching.

Unofficially, however, overnight camping is usually tolerated, so long as you pitch a small tent unobtrusively in the evening, and pack up and leave early the next morning, without leaving a trace.

Alternatively, there are popular luggage transfer services on the more established stretches of the Path. For a small fee, they will pick up your rucksack and other bags and transport them to the end of your day's walk. A list of luggage transfer companies appears at the back of the book.

Clothes, boots and backpack

For those new to long distance walking, it's worth emphasising the benefits of comfortable walking boots and suitable clothing. Walking continuously, day after day, puts extra pressures on your feet. Be prepared for changes in the weather, too. Carry waterproofs and remember that several thin layers allow you to adjust your clothing as conditions change.

Checking the weather forecast before you set off each day will help you decide what to wear. If you're in the car, it's worth taking a selection of clothing for different conditions, and deciding what to wear and carry immediately before you start.

Onshore breezes can mask the strength of the sun. To avoid sunburn, or even sunstroke, remember to slap on some sunscreen and wear a hat.

Other things to take, depending on weight, include: maps, water bottle, lightweight walking poles, basic First Aid including plasters and antiseptic cream, penknife, head torch and spare batteries, chocolate, sweets or energy bars, toilet paper, a small camera, binoculars, mobile phone, and a pen and notebook. Don't forget some spare cash too; most places accept cards but finding a Cashpoint or somewhere that offers 'Cash Back' near the Path can be tricky.

Pembrokeshire's Barafundle Bay is one of the UK's finest beaches

Sea fortress: *Llansteffan Castle guards the Tâf Estuary on Carmarthen Bay*

Food and drink
Although the official guidebooks try to start and end each day at places with amenities, some sections are nonetheless remote and may have few places to buy food or drink. This may be the case for several days in a row. So it makes sense to plan ahead and carry enough supplies with you.

Conversely, other sections are well supplied with shops, pubs, cafés, restaurants and takeaways, and these are indicated at the start of each Day Section.

Maps
The maps in this book are based on the Ordnance Survey Landranger 1:50,000 series, with the line of the Wales Coast Path highlighted in orange. The numbers on the maps correspond to those in the route description for each day section.

The best maps for walking are the larger scale, orange-covered Ordnance Survey Explorer 1:25,000 scale maps, which show additional features such as Access Land, field boundaries, springs and wells. Both scales of OS maps now have the official route of the Wales Coast Path marked on them: as a line composed of a series of red diamonds on the 1:50,000 Landranger maps, and green diamonds on the 1:25,000 Explorer maps.

The relevant maps for each Day Section are listed at the beginning of each chapter. The grid references given in this book for the start and finish of each Day Section are from the Ordnance Survey maps.

Route finding

For the most part, the Wales Coast Path follows a single official route. In a few places, there are both official and unofficial alternative routes. Otherwise, the path hugs the coast as far is practically and legally possible, occasionally diverting inland around private estates, nature reserves, natural obstacles, estuaries, gunnery ranges and so on. The definitive route, and any occasional changes are notified on the official Wales Coast Path website.

The path uses a mixture of public rights of way: footpaths, bridleways and byways as well as lanes, open access land, beaches and some permissive paths. On most sections, the route is well-used and clear. In remote or under-used areas, however, walkers will need to pay closer attention to the maps and directions in this book.

The beautiful Three Cliffs Bay, Gower

Way to go: *Oak posts and waymarkers with the Wales Coast Path symbol mark the route*

Fingerposts and waymarkers

The Wales Coast Path is clearly signed and waymarked with its own distinctive logo: a white dragon-tailed seashell on a blue background surrounded by a yellow circlet bearing the words *'Llwybr Arfordir Cymru - Wales Coast Path'*. Look for the wood or metal fingerposts at main access points, in towns, on roadsides and lanes, and at key junctions.

Official route waymarkers *Official alternative route waymarkers*

Elsewhere the route is clearly waymarked with plastic roundels fixed to stiles, gateposts, fences and walls. In many places the Wales Coast Path waymarkers sit alongside others for already established routes — such as the Isle of Anglesey Coastal Path or the Pembrokeshire Coast Path National Trail. In some areas these local waymarkers are still more in evidence than the official Wales Coast Path ones; and on some stretches, waymarking remains patchy.

Alternative routes

Two sorts of alternative route are described in the guides. The first are the **official alternative routes** that avoid remote or challenging sections; and more attractive routes that, for example, provide better views or get farther away from motor traffic.

The second are our own **unofficial alternative routes**. Many of these are beach routes below the high water mark that by their nature are not permanently available, and so do not qualify as part of the 'official route'. Others are alternative high level routes or simply 'better' or more attractive, in our opinion. Both the **official** and **unofficial alternative routes** are shown on the maps in this book as a broken orange highlight.

Detours

The directions also describe **detours** to places of interest that we think you won't want to miss. These are usually short, off the main Path, there-and-back routes, typically of no more than a kilometre or so in each direction. Suggested detours can take you to anything from a special pub, castle or church to a stunning view or waterfall. If you've got the time, they bring an extra dimension to the walk. Detours are shown as a blue broken highlight.

Temporary diversions

There may be occasional or seasonal temporary inland diversions. The reasons for them vary from land management and public safety: forestry work, cliff falls, landslips and floods, to wildlife conservation: protecting seal breeding sites, bird roosts and nesting sites, and so on. Details of the latest permanent and temporary diversions can be found on the official Wales Coast Path website under 'Route Changes'. See **www.walescoastpath.gov.uk.**

Tides and tide tables

As much as five percent of the Wales Coast Path runs along the foreshore, between mean high and low water. These sections are naturally affected by the tide. On the whole, the official Wales Coast Path avoids beaches and estuaries. However, beaches often provide time-honoured, direct and pleasant walking routes and are usually safely accessible, except for around 1½ hours either side of high tide. If the tide is in, or you're in any doubt, take the inland route instead.

Occasional streams and tidal creeks may also be crossed at low tide but be impassable at high water. So it is a good idea to carry tide tables with you and consult them before you set out each day. They are widely available for around £1 from coastal TICs, shops and newsagents.

Ancient layers: *Limestone cliffs at Nash Point on the Glamorgan Heritage Coast, South Wales*

Several websites also give accurate tidal predictions for locations around the UK, including downloadable five day predictions. Useful websites include: **www.bbc.co.uk/weather/coast_and_sea/tide_tables** and **www.ukho.gov.uk/easytide**.

Safety advice

If you're new to long-distance walking, or in one of the remoter areas, please remember:

- Wear walking boots and warm, waterproof clothing.
- Take food and drink.
- Mobile signals are patchy along much of the Path; let someone know where you are heading and when you expect to arrive.
- If you decide to walk along a beach, always check tide tables.
- Stay on the path and away from cliff edges.
- Take extra care in windy and/or wet conditions.
- Always supervise children and dogs.
- Follow local signs and diversions.

Emergencies

In an emergency, call 999 or 112 and ask for the service you require: Ambulance, Police, Fire or Coastguard.

Tell them your location as accurately as possible (give an OS grid reference, if possible; and look for named landmarks), how many people are in your party, and the nature of the problem.

Remember, though, that mobile signals may be poor or absent in some areas. Some coastal car parks and main beach access points have emergency telephones. Coastal pubs and shops may also have phones you can ask to use in an emergency.

Who manages the Path?

The Wales Coast Path is co-ordinated at a national level by Natural Resources Wales and managed on the ground by the sixteen local authorities and two National Parks through which it passes.

Funding has come from the Welsh Government, the European Regional Development Fund and the local authorities themselves.

For more details, see: **http://naturalresourceswales.gov.uk**

The Best of the South Wales Coast

The South Wales section of the Wales Coast Path is surprisingly detached from the busyness of the M4 corridor. Along the way are four National Nature Reserves and some 14 miles of designated Heritage Coast, while the deserted salt marshes and mudflats bordering the later stages of the route alongside the mouth of the River Severn are a bird-watchers' paradise. Much of the grim 19th- and early 20th-century industry of the coastal ports has gone, replaced partly by regeneration but elsewhere reclaimed for nature and recreation. New habitats are attracting rarities in plant and animal life; seals, salmon, otters and even the elusive bittern are making a comeback.

Dylan Thomas sculpture, Swansea

Kenfig Pool

Ogmore Castle

Dunraven Bay

Nash Point

Llantwit Major

Cardiff Bay

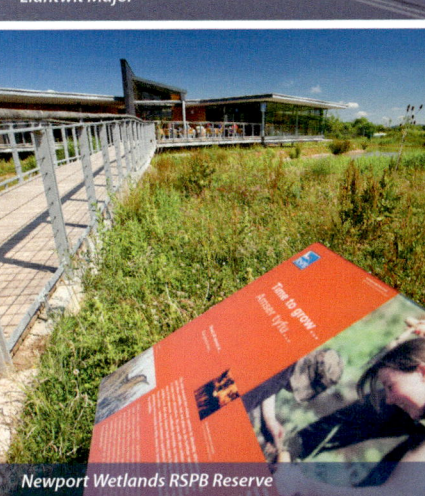
Newport Wetlands RSPB Reserve

Second Severn Crossing

Chepstow Castle

The South Wales Coast
Part of the Wales Coast Path

Despite the massive industrialisation and urbanisation of the 19th and early 20th centuries, much of the **south coast of Wales** remains surprisingly unspoilt and harbours a tremendous wildlife and recreational resource that sits on the doorstep for much of the country's population. And those from afar, whose only knowledge of the area has been gleaned from the history of coal, iron and steel, will certainly be stunned by the great open sweeps of fine beaches, great dune systems, impressive cliffs, tidal salt marshes and reclaimed meadowlands, all of which revel in a profusion of wildflowers, insects, birds and animal life. Unexpected though such sea and landscapes might be from a quick glance at the map, these are the predominant environments through which this last section of the Wales Coast Path runs.

There are many ancient hillforts along this section of Welsh coast, many protected by Cadw. Even so, there is no ignoring the industrial conurbations of Swansea, Port Talbot, Barry, Cardiff and Newport. But the commercial activity of the 21st century now looks towards high tech, specialised manufacture and the service and media industries. Reclamation and redevelopment of

Walkers on the Glamorgan Heritage Coast

derelict and brownfield sites has removed much of the detrimental impact of the old industries on the environment and new areas have been deliberately set aside for open space and nature. Hidden gems worth exploring include the Newport Wetlands and Kenfig Pool and dunes. In keeping close to the coast, there are inevitably occasional sections of street walking, but these can be avoided, either by following striking inland routes or opting for a short bus ride. Yet even the abandoned 'edgelands' hold surprises, for this is where nature appears at its most feral. The plants here are the advance guard of natural regeneration, overcoming harsh conditions and bringing insects and birds in their wake.

This final section of the Wales Coast Path may not portray the absolute wildness of Pembrokeshire's Atlantic-battered cliffs or the dramatic scenery of the Snowdonian fringe, but it is equally full of character and merit. Nature's offerings are abundant and diverse, and the relics of industrial heritage give a wonderful insight into a past that helped make Wales great.

"Travel and change of place impart new vigour to the mind."

Seneca, *Roman Stoic philosopher, 4 BC – AD 65*

Wales Coast Path: SOUTH WALES COAST

Day Section	Distance	Start	Finish
Day Section 1 Swansea to Port Talbot	11 miles 18 km	Swansea Barrage SS 665 926	Port Talbot SS 759 896
Day Section 2 Port Talbot to Porthcawl	11½ miles 18.5 km	Port Talbot SS 759 896	Porthcawl Point SS 818 765
Day Section 3 Porthcawl to Ogmore	9 miles 14.5 km	Porthcawl Point SS 818 765	Ogmore by Sea SS 861 755
Day Section 4 Ogmore to Llantwit Major	10 miles 16 km	Ogmore by Sea SS 861 755	Col-huw Point SS 956 674

Walking the South Wales Coast

The South Wales Coast section of the Wales Coast Path runs for 115 miles/185 kilometres between the River Tawe at Swansea to the River Wye at Chepstow.

This guide divides the path into nine logical Day Sections that range between 9 – 19 miles/15 – 30 kilometres. All start or finish within reach of facilities and/or are close to transport links. The Day Sections are shown on the chart and map above.

South Wales Coast Part of the Wales Coast Path

Day Section	Distance	Start	Finish
Day Section 5 Llantwit Major to Barry Island	12 miles 19.5 km	Col-huw Point SS 956 674	Barry Island ST 106 668
Day Section 6 Barry Island to Cardiff Barrage	15 miles 24 km	Barry Island ST 106 668	Cardiff Barrage ST 190 724
Day Section 7 Cardiff Barrage to Newport	20¾ miles 33.5 km	Cardiff Barrage ST 190 724	Newport ST 316 862
Day Section 8 Newport to Redwick	12 miles 19.5 km	Newport ST 316 862	Redwick ST 416 834
Day Section 9 Redwick to Chepstow	14¼ miles 23 km	Redwick ST 416 834	Chepstow ST 536 942

Distance chart for key locations along the path

Miles (upper-right triangle) / **Kilometres** (lower-left triangle). Distances are approximate to the nearest mile/kilometre.

From ↓ / To →	Chepstow	Mathern	Sudbrook	Caldicot	Severn Tunnel Junction	Newport Wetlands	Newport Pillgwenlly	Lighthouse Park	Cardiff Parc Treddelerch	Cardiff Bay	Penarth	Sully	Barry	Barry Island	Rhoose	Gileston	Cwm Colhuw	Dunraven Bay	Ogmore-by-Sea	Porthcawl	Margam	Port Talbot	Baglan	Swansea River Tawe
Swansea River Tawe	112	108	106	103	102	89	84	78	72	67	64	58	55	52	47	43	39	32	29	21	15	12	6	
Baglan	106	102	100	97	96	83	78	73	66	61	58	52	49	46	41	37	33	26	23	15	9	6		10
Port Talbot	100	96	93	91	90	77	72	66	60	55	52	46	42	40	35	31	27	20	17	9	3		10	19
Margam	97	93	90	88	87	74	69	63	57	52	49	43	39	37	32	28	24	17	14	6		5	15	24
Porthcawl	91	87	85	82	81	68	63	58	51	46	43	37	34	31	26	22	18	11	8		9	14	24	34
Ogmore-by-Sea	83	79	76	74	73	60	55	49	43	38	35	29	25	23	17	14	10	3		13	23	28	38	47
Dunraven Bay	81	76	74	71	70	57	52	47	41	36	33	26	23	20	15	12	7		4	17	27	32	42	51
Cwm Colhuw	74	69	67	64	63	50	45	40	34	29	25	19	16	13	8	4		11	15	29	38	43	53	63
Gileston	69	65	62	60	59	46	41	35	29	24	21	15	11	9	3		7	19	23	36	45	50	60	70
Rhoose	66	62	59	56	55	42	37	32	26	21	18	12	8	5		5	13	24	28	41	51	56	66	75
Barry Island	61	56	54	51	50	37	32	27	21	15	12	6	3		8	14	21	32	36	50	59	64	74	83
Barry	58	54	51	48	48	34	29	24	18	13	10	4		4	13	18	25	37	41	54	64	68	78	88
Sully	54	50	47	45	44	31	26	20	14	9	6		6	10	19	24	31	43	47	60	69	74	84	94
Penarth	48	44	41	39	38	25	20	14	8	3		10	16	20	28	34	41	52	56	70	79	84	94	103
Cardiff Bay	45	41	38	36	35	22	17	11	5		5	15	20	25	33	39	46	57	61	75	84	89	99	108
Cardiff Parc Treddelerch	40	36	33	31	30	17	11	6		8	13	23	29	33	41	47	54	65	69	83	92	97	107	117
Lighthouse Park	34	30	27	25	24	11	5		10	18	23	33	38	43	51	57	64	75	79	93	102	107	117	126
Newport Pillgwenlly	29	24	22	19	18	5		9	18	27	31	41	47	51	60	65	72	84	88	101	111	115	125	135
Newport Wetlands	23	19	17	14	13		8	17	27	35	40	50	55	60	68	74	81	92	96	110	119	124	134	143
Severn Tunnel Junction	10	6	3	1		21	29	38	48	56	61	71	76	81	89	95	102	113	117	131	140	145	155	164
Caldicot	9	5	2		2	23	31	40	49	58	62	72	78	82	91	96	103	115	119	132	142	146	156	166
Sudbrook	7	3		4	6	27	35	44	53	62	66	76	82	86	95	100	107	119	123	136	146	150	160	170
Mathern	4		4	8	10	31	39	48	58	66	71	80	86	91	99	104	112	123	127	140	150	161	165	174
Chepstow		7	11	15	17	38	46	55	64	73	77	87	93	97	106	111	118	130	134	147	157	167	171	181

Distances are approximate to the nearest mile/kilometre

Day Sections

1: Swansea (River Tawe) to Port Talbot

Distance: 11 miles/18 kilometres (upland alternative - 10 miles/16 kilometres)

Terrain: Although the lowland route is generally flat and includes significant stretches beside roads, there are surprising gems to contradict the common perceptions of this industrial area. Leaving Swansea, the route skirts a nature reserve beside a quiet and lovely disused canal, then beyond Briton Ferry, crosses extensive marsh and dunes to the beach and promenade at Aberavon. Alternatively, an upland route between Briton Ferry and Port Talbot climbs behind the coastal plain to find quiet paths across wooded slopes, injecting a mild challenge of occasional ups and downs — and some great views of the coast and its industrial heritage.

Points of interest: Swansea Marina and National Waterfront Museum, Dylan Thomas Centre, Swansea Docks, Dylan Thomas Birth Place and Cwmdonkin Park, Tennant Canal and Crymlyn Bog Nature Reserve, 1940s Swansea, dunes, Aberavon Sands, Mynydd Forest.

Note: Tourist Information — see: www.visitswanseabay.com; major transport links, accommodation, shops, post office, banks and refreshment at both Swansea and Port Talbot.

Swansea Marina and docks from the air

2: Port Talbot to Porthcawl

Distance: 11½ miles/18.5 kilometres (upland alternative 14 miles/22.5 kilometres)

Terrain: Again barred from the coast by docks and industry, the lowland course to Margam follows roads and urban streets and is predictably uninspiring. However, a more strenuous alternative offers a delightful escape onto open hillsides from which there are fine views across the coastal plain. The two ways come together to cross Margam Moors and the fringe of Kenfig Sands, where there is generally easy walking through an arresting wetland and dune habitat.

Points of interest: Second World War radar station, Margam Abbey, Margam Stones museum, Margam Country Park, Kenfig Burrows, Rest Bay, Porthcawl Harbour

Note: Major transport links serve Port Talbot, with bus services to Porthcawl. Accommodation, shops, post office, banks and refreshment in both towns.

3: Porthcawl to Ogmore

Distance: 9 miles/ 14.5 kilometres

Terrain: Beyond the streets of Porthcawl, there's easy walking through pleasant dunes and woodland for most of the section, with just a couple of stretches beside quiet lanes.

The wildlife-rich sand dunes at Kenfig Burrows

One step at a time: *The stepping stones below Ogmore Castle (Not on the WCP Official Route)*

Points of interest: Merthyr-mawr Warren, Merthyr-mawr church, Ogmore Castle, Candleston Castle, Ewenny Priory, WW2 fortifications

Note: No facilities beyond Porthcawl. The official route uses the bridge over the Ewenny River; if using the stepping stones downstream by the castle, remember these are flooded at high water.

4: Ogmore to Col-huw/Llantwit Major

Distance: 10 miles/ 16 kilometres

Terrain: Clifftop path all the way with several steep gradients and occasional opportunities to reach the beach.

Points of interest: Stunning Heritage Coast, Heritage Centre, Dunraven Estate, St Donat's Castle and Arts Centre, St Donat's Church, Llantwit Major, Iron Age coastal forts

Note: Post office, shop and visitor information in Ogmore village; toilets and seasonal cafés at Dunraven Bay, Nash Point and Col-huw, accommodation and pubs at Southerndown and Monknash; pub at Marcross; accommodation, toilets, shops, post office, banks, refreshment and bus and rail links at Llantwit Major

Heritage Coast: *The fossil-rich Carboniferous limestone cliffs near Nash Point*

5: Col-huw/Llantwit Major to Barry Island

Distance: 12 miles/ 19.5 kilometres

Terrain: Clifftop path with occasional steep gradients to Aberthaw. The onward path is constrained along the sea wall around Aberthaw Power Station, but reverts to open coast and cliff walking around Rhoose until the promenade at The Knap. The circuit of Barry Island incorporates promenade paths and urban streets, passing both its fine beaches.

Points of interest: Iron Age coastal forts, Roman remains, Porthkerry Country Park, southern-most point of Wales, industrial lime kilns, Barry Island resort

Note: Accommodation at West Aberthaw and Gileston; pubs at Porthkerry, St Athan and Fontygary; café and toilets at Porthkerry Country Park; visitor information, accommodation, toilets, shops, post office, banks, refreshment and bus and rail links at Barry Island

6: Barry Island to Cardiff Barrage

Distance: 15 miles/ 24 kilometres

Terrain: The urban and industrial access roads encircling Barry Docks to the

coast at Sully can be avoided by a bus ride, but the route beyond is pleasant and largely follows coastal paths above a low, rocky shore to Penarth.

Points of interest: Lavernock Point, Sully Island, Penarth Pier and Pavilion, WW2 fortifications, Marconi's Tower

Note: Accommodation, shops, cafes and restaurants, post office, banks, bus and rail links at Barry and Penarth; toilets, restaurants and café at Swanbridge

7: Cardiff Barrage to Newport (Transporter Bridge)

Distance: 20¾ miles / 33.5 kilometres, (or 18½ miles/30 kilometres using the Transporter Bridge)

Terrain: The vibrant Cardiff Bay waterfront and Atlantic Wharf development present an exciting view of Wales' capital city. However, many will find the subsequent urban and industrial access roads skirting Cardiff Docks less appealing and may opt to take the bus, either to East Moors or Tremorfa. Beyond, is the Parc Tredelerch nature reserve before following the ancient flood defences protecting the coastal levels of Peterstone and Wentlooge to Newport. Time your journey to coincide with the Transporter Bridge opening to avoid a lengthy main-road detour over the road bridge (bus alternative).

Gold and silver: *The Millennium Centre and Roald Dahl Square, Cardiff*

Points of interest: Cardiff Bay and its Barrage, National Museum and Cathays Park, St Fagans National History Museum, Tredelerch Park, coast, West Usk Lighthouse, Newport Transporter Bridge, National Roman Legion Museum Caerleon

Note: Visitor Information Point at Cardiff Castle; accommodation, shops, post office, banks, refreshment and bus and rail links at Cardiff; pub at St Brides Wentlooge, where there is also accommodation; Tourist Information Centre, accommodation, shops, post office, banks, refreshment and bus and rail links at Newport.

8: Newport (Transporter Bridge) to Redwick

Distance: 12 miles/ 19.5 kilometres

Terrain: Riverside and field paths then offer a surprisingly pleasant route out of town to the coastal levels and on to Redwick.

Points of interest: RSPB Newport Wetlands National Nature Reserve, East Usk Lighthouse, Redwick church

Note: Few amenities en route but there are pubs at Nash, Goldcliff and Redwick, and a café at Uskmouth RSPB Reserve. There are bus services through Nash and Goldcliff and accommodation at Nash and Redwick.

9: Redwick to Chepstow

Distance: 14¼ miles/ 23 kilometres

Terrain: Easy walking along the coastal levels, before following field paths to the outskirts of Chepstow. Streets and urban parks take the final section into the town centre.

Points of interest: Coastal Levels, Chepstow, castle, walls, museum and wharves, Mathern church, The Severn Bridges, Bulwark fort, Sudbrook and Severn Tunnel

Note: Few amenities en route, bus and rail links at Severn Tunnel Junction; Tourist Information Centre, accommodation, shops, post office, banks, refreshment and bus and rail links at Chepstow

Chepstow Castle crouches on high cliffs above the Wye

Limited for time? — The South Wales Coast in a nutshell

If you have only a limited time to explore this section of the Wales Coast Path, then these key parts of the path are unmissable.

If you visit nowhere else in South Wales, Cardiff Bay is a must. It stands at the heart of Wales' capital city, a brilliant focus for the region's cultural, historic, leisure and economic diversity that incorporates a stunning wetland nature reserve. The Cardiff Bay Trail is a stunning 6 mile/10 kilometre route that follows the waterfront around the vast freshwater bay.

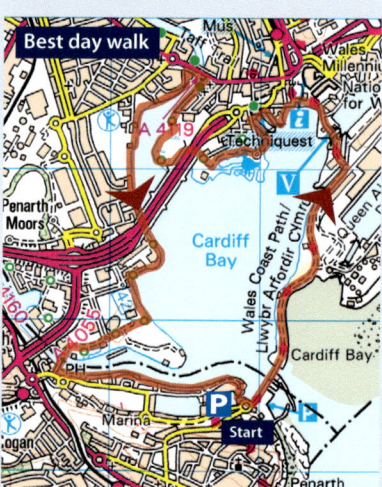

With another two days to spare, follow the coast path from the mouth of the Ogmore River to Barry Island. The stretch includes the Glamorgan Heritage Coast and the southernmost point of mainland Wales at Rhoose Point. The ancient monastic town of Llantwit Major provides a convenient overnight stop and there's the promise of fish and chips on the beach at Barry Island at the end.

Best day walk

Trace the waterfront around Cardiff Bay in the heart of Wales' first city

Cardiff Bay Trail: 6 miles/10 kilometres

Completed for the millennium, the Barrage transformed the tidal estuary of Tiger Bay into a massive freshwater lake with a spectacular waterfront promenade. Park in the large pay and display car park by the Barrage locks below Penarth and follow the circular path past the restored docks, across the Taff and Ely rivers and back past the Penarth Marina.

Cardiff Bay waterfront

Best weekend walk

The Glamorgan Heritage Coast and the southern-most point of Wales

Ogmore to Barry Island: 25 miles/40 kilometres

Day One: Start at Ogmore-by-Sea (Day Section 3), but first look upriver at Ogmore Castle. Highlights include the Heritage Coast Centre and Nash Point lighthouses before heading inland via Cwm Col-huw to Llantwit Major.

Day Two: Explore the old town then return to the coast and continue west past Aberthaw and Rhoose Point to Barry Island. Don't miss the old limeworks at Aberthaw, Porthkerry Church and the Roman remains at The Knap. There are car parks at Ogmore and Barry Island, while the train and a short bus journey link the two.

Nash Point, Glamorgan Heritage Coast

A brief history of the South Wales Coast

Man's history has moulded the landscape of South Wales more than anywhere else on the coast

Twelve thousand years ago, a warming climate banished a mantle of ice from the shores of Britain, creating opportunities that our expansionist Stone Age ancestors were quick to exploit. The long south coast of Wales looked very different then, but must have seemed a bounteous place to roaming bands of hunter-gatherers, paddling up the Bristol Channel into the Severn Estuary. These folk were highly skilled at hunting, fishing and living off the land and here, somewhat sheltered from the worst of the Atlantic storms, they found great stretches of tidal salt marsh, teeming with the easy pickings of abundant water fowl, molluscs and fish. The woods and clearings of the back marsh attracted game such as boar, deer and auroch, while the banks of drier ground were ideal sites for seasonal camps.

St Lythan's Neolithic burial chamber, Vale of Glamorgan

For the most part, traces of everyday lives are scant and hidden beneath deep layers of silt washed in by the tides. Archaeology has revealed finds of stone tools (often traded over great distances), shell middens and the scars of butchery on animal bones, but truly evocative are footprints occasionally exposed on the foreshore mud of low tides.

The first farmers

The Mesolithic way of life was gradually superseded by the development of agriculture and husbandry. Clearing fields from the hinterland forest was an investment that tied communities to a place, a permanence reflected in the construction of monumental ceremonial burial cairns. At St Lythans, some four miles inland from Barry is an impressive Neolithic cromlech, while the burial chamber at nearby Tinkinswood is one of the finest in the country. Some 6,000 years old, they demand a short excursion from the route.

The seemingly peaceful farming way of life continued, aided by the appearance of copper and then bronze implements around 2100 BC. Pottery artefacts from about this period have been recovered from a hut site found near Magor, while part of a sewn-plank boat was discovered at Goldcliff.

A cooler climate from around 1200 BC appears to have imposed stress on society, intensifying competition for resources. Iron gradually replaced bronze, enabling weapons and tools that were both harder and capable of sustaining a sharper edge. An increase of weaponry is seen in the archaeological finds and, from about 800 BC, defended settlement sites or 'hillforts' began to appear, with several examples sited on the higher ground behind the South Wales coast.

Celts and Romans

But even so, the resistance of the native Silures proved little match for the Romans, who bridged the Wye above Chepstow around AD 48. Advancing across South Wales, they established a major fort at Carleon and a civil trading town at Caer-went, with the major river estuaries further west serving as landings for sea trade along the Bristol Channel and from the continent. The foundations of a Roman coastal building have been found at Porthkerry and it was the Romans who began fundamentally changing the landscape with the reclamation of marshes east of the Rhymney River using reens (drainage ditches) to create new farmland.

Ogmore Castle's Grade I listed ruined keep

Fallen arches: *The 850-year old ruins of Margam Abbey*

Missionaries and Normans

The Roman abandonment of Britain at the end of the 4th century left the coast vulnerable to raiders, but there soon developed close ties with Ireland as Celtic Christianity spread along the western European seaboard. Many inlets and landings have traditional links with the early saints and monastic communities were established at numerous places including Baglan, Margam, Merthyr Mawr, Monknash, Llantwit and Barry.

In 1066, the Normans landed at Hastings and within a year had established a border castle at Chepstow. Over time, other castles followed to oversee the estuary landings further west and during the medieval period a distinctive Cambro-Norman society developed, which prospered from trade along the coast and further afield.

With the Normans had come a new wave of monastic foundation and endowment and it was often they, particularly Margam, Goldcliff and Tintern (which lay up the Wye Valley), who oversaw the recovery and augmentation of the work begun by the Romans in extending grazing and farmland across the marshes.

Drama after dark: *Smoke and lights enliven the South Wales' steelworks at night*

Underground riches

The real source of wealth, however, lay in the iron and coal buried in the hills behind the coast, something hardly exploited before the 18th century when the need for cannon to defend British world interests and the burgeoning Industrial Revolution created an unprecedented demand for iron. Supply was hampered, not by resources but a lack of effective transport and it awaited canals and then railways linking the valleys to the ports for the industry to really take off.

For a while, Wales, with its pure ore, held a near monopoly of steel-making, but Gilchrist's discovery in 1876 that adding limestone to the process removed the phosphorous that made steel brittle meant ore from almost anywhere could be used. Production shifted from Merthry Tydfil and the other iron towns to the coast where cheaper, foreign ore could be landed.

Coal (known as 'Black Gold' in Wales), became an important export in its own right, fuelling the steam engines of industry, railways and shipping across the world and the ports vied with each other for the trade, building ever-larger docks. South Wales quickly dominated the coal market and its ports were amongst the busiest in the world.

Change and change again

The whole coast was crowded with shipping: great ships travelling between the farthest corners of Empire, coastal traders moving goods from port to port and sedate passenger vessels taking day-trippers back and forth along the Bristol Channel. The 19th century had seen the transition from horse, sail and waterpower to steam, with Welsh coal accounting for the greater proportion of all that used world-wide, but as a new century dawned, the balance gradually began to change in favour of oil. Despite the transient booms in production caused by two world wars, the ports began a slow decline and the latter decades of the 20th century saw the virtual end of Welsh coal.

Yet, nothing stands still; wind, wave and tide are emerging as new energy sources while the export of Welsh coal has been replaced by imports of natural gas and wood. The economy of South Wales is adapting to the new order, becoming more eco-friendly and even creating fresh environments for nature to embrace.

Wildlife along the South Wales Coast

Walking the **Wales Coast Path** is a journey though a succession of different wildlife habitats: beaches, cliffs, dunes, estuary and salt marsh, each with the potential to reveal something new. The constantly changing weather and progression of the seasons add other perspectives, leaving no two days the same. There's a wonderful stretch of Heritage Coast and a couple of National Nature Reserves — with local reserves, conservation areas and open country in between. Flowers, insects, birds and small animals are to be found everywhere, and sometimes pop up in the most unexpected corners. So keep your eyes open and don't write off the urban fringes as a wasteland.

Bearded tit

Dune pansy

Sea asters

Peregrine

Heritage coast, sand dunes and reclaimed nature reserves

The South Wales Coast's dune systems, limestone cliffs and estuarine saltmarshes and mudflats are rich in wildlife

Don't believe all you might have read or heard about South Wales: it's certainly not all coalmines, iron foundries and steel works. The coast (and indeed much of the mountain and valley hinterland too) is predominantly open countryside, unspoiled by the economic and urban pressures of modern life. Cliffs, estuaries, salt marshes and dune systems offer some of the most rewarding wildlife habitats in the country and you'll find these and more spread along the length of the South Wales coast.

Surprisingly, many of the sites once blighted by heavy industry: sprawling factories and warehouses, plant, transport routes and tips and dumps for waste and slag, have been transformed and now host a variety of less common plant species including uncommon orchids and marsh helleborine. Where a few plants find a toehold, others follow, attracting insects, birds and other wildlife. The proof that the abandoned industrial sites of yesterday

The dunes at Merthyr-mawr are the highest in northern Europe

can truly become the nature reserves of tomorrow is vividly demonstrated here in South Wales.

Priceless dune systems

One of the country's most fragile environment types are dune systems, where prevailing winds pile up sand washed in by the sea, the whole system gradually creeping inland. These form the long run of coast from Crymlyn Burrows to the scoop of Merthyr-mawr Warren beside the estuary of the Ogmore River, much of it a designated SSSI. It is a 'living system', its nature changing as it becomes colonised by a progression of plants ranging from couch and marram grasses to eventual woodland, each adapted to a different set of conditions.

Amongst the 300 or so different plants to be found are sand cat's tail, petalwort, red fescue, rock sea lavender, hutchinsia, dune pansy and rest harrow and, where woodland has developed, there are many varieties of fungi. The dunes attract a wide range of insects; look out for different types of bee and Britain's largest cricket, the great green bush cricket, which can be over 2½ inches long.

Glamorgan Heritage Coast

About one-third of the Welsh coast is designated 'Heritage Coast' with a wonderful run of 14 miles here in South Wales between Ogmore and Aberthaw. Its impressively striated cliffs attract not only nesting seabirds such as fulmar but also ravens, jackdaws and even the unmistakably red booted chough, which are steadily increasing in numbers.

Despite their name, the natural homes of house martins are cliffs and in early summer you'll find them around Nash Point. Other smaller birds include the stonechat, which you'll more often hear than see, its call a sharp rap like two stones being knocked together. Look out too for hunting peregrine falcons, though they will be just as happy finding a perch on one of Cardiff's tall city-centre buildings.

Down on the beach at Dunraven when the tide is out, search out clumps of honeycomb reef which are created by colonies of small worms from particles of sand shell. At high water they wave tentacles from the openings to catch plankton. In the pools around the reef wave-washed platform you'll find anemones, crabs and molluscs.

Back on the downs above, keep an eye open for one of Glamorgan's rarities, the high brown fritillary butterfly. More common though are brown hares, which can appear at any time of year.

Breeding peregrines hunt along the Glamorgan Heritage Coast

Rare beauty: *Marsh helleborines flourish in South Wales' lime-rich dune systems*

Reclaimed for nature

The former ash tips and abandoned limestone quarries beyond Aberthaw are fine examples of how nature can recover an industrial landscape. Rare orchids, helleborines and autumn lady's tresses populate the chalky grasslands while yellow horned poppies sprout amongst the shingle and purple gromwell fringes areas of scrub. Another rarity is the true service tree, which has been found in the woods cloaking the cliffs towards Porthkerry. On the foreshore, the intertidal rocks are home to barnacles, periwinkles, limpets and seaweeds and the saline pools harbour the curious flat worm.

Around Lavernock Point Nature Reserve, the old hay fields are rich in summer meadow flowers, such as devils' bit scabious, orchids, cowslip. In fact, more than 170 species have been logged. These attract numerous butterflies and moths among which are purple hairstreak, gatekeeper and ringlet. It is also a favourite spot for birdwatchers.

Cardiff may be the biggest city in Wales, but is not wildlife desert. Although the construction of the Barrage flooded a vast expanse of tidal marsh, a wetland reserve has been created at the northern end. Since the Barrage closed in 2001, the vegetation has progressively shifted from saline to fresh water species. Amongst the birds visiting the reeds are warblers and reed bunting as well as grey herons and ducks.

Waterworld?: *Otters hunt for fish in the marshes and reedbeds, and along coastal reens*

Grazing marsh and wetlands

Running for some 20 miles beyond Cardiff are the Wentlooge and Caldicot levels, one of the largest areas of grazing marsh left in Britain and consequently much of it is designated as SSSI and other biodiversity protections as part of the Severn Estuary. Criss-crossed by a network of drainage reens and dotted with reedy pools, it is teeming with plant and wildlife amongst which are several rare or uncommon species. Water voles and otters move freely along the many miles of ditches, whose banks are thick with reeds, flag iris and teasel. The water also attracts dragonflies such as the common darter and the southern hawker whilst above the rich flower meadows dance countless butterflies including tortoiseshell, painted lady, peacock and skippers.

At the heart of the levels, beside the Usk estuary, lies the Newport Wetlands RSPB Reserve, which provides a focus for finding out about the ecology of the area and the variety of life it supports. Particular successes on the reserve are sightings of bittern and the establishment of breeding colonies of avocet and bearded tits, the latter actually a 'parrot bill' and not a 'tit' at all. Autumn and winter is a particularly rewarding time to visit the area since the extensive mudflats exposed at low tide are feeding grounds for thousands of overwintering waterfowl and waders. Amongst them are dunlin, redshank and curlews, whilst Canada geese flock on the fields behind.

Expect the unexpected

The sheer variety of landscapes along this final section of the Wales Coast Path guarantees something new around each corner and at any time of year there will undoubtedly be much to delight any nature lover. With many surprises and unusual sightings it pays to have a good pocket field guide and pair of binoculars to hand.

Of course, the above is only a brief summary of the range of wildlife that may be encountered along this section of the Wales Coast Path. For further details about the region's natural heritage, check out the Natural Resources Wales website at **www.naturalresourceswales.gov.uk**

Avocets sift for food in shallow pools along the South Wales Coast

Day Sections

1. Swansea (River Tawe) to Port Talbot *11 miles/ 18 kilometres*
2. Port Talbot to Porthcawl *11½ miles/ 18.5 kilometres*
3. Porthcawl to Ogmore *9 miles/ 14.5 kilometres*
4. Ogmore to Llantwit Major *10 miles/ 16 kilometres*
5. Llantwit Major to Barry *12 miles/ 19.5 kilometres*
6. Barry to Cardiff Bay *15 miles/ 24 kilometres*
7. Cardiff Bay to Newport (Transporter Bridge) *20¾ miles/ 33.5 kilometres*
8. Newport (Transporter Bridge) to Redwick *12 miles/ 19.5 kilometres*
9. Redwick to Chepstow *14¼ miles/ 23 kilometres*

The South Wales Coast section of the Wales Coast Path

Stepping stones below Ogmore Castle (Day Section 3)

SECTION ONE

Swansea to Port Talbot

Distance: *11 miles / 18 kilometres (Alternative 10 miles / 16 kilometres)* | **Start:** *Swansea Barrage SS 665 926* | **Finish:** *A4241 roundabout SS 759 896 (alternative – Tesco roundabout SS 766 902)* | **Maps:** *OS Landrangers 159 Swansea & Gower and 170 Vale of Glamorgan or OS Explorer 165 Swansea*

Outline: Redeveloped docks and canal followed by beach or open hillside offer enjoyable countryside escapes in this otherwise built-up area.

Docks and industrial development push the path from the coast but the first leg meets open countryside along the towpath of the disused Tennant Canal past the Crymlyn Bog Nature Reserve. After an unavoidable stretch of main road to Briton Ferry there's a choice between the dunes and open beach of Aberavon Sands or a foray onto the slopes of the wooded hills overlooking Baglan. At Port Talbot, a pedestrian link path through the town centre connects the two routes.

Services: *Swansea and Port Talbot offer a range of accommodation and support services, with toilets at the bus and rail stations and on Aberavon promenade. There's food en route in Swansea Docks, Briton Ferry roundabout and on Aberavon promenade as well as a superstore in Port Talbot. For tourist information, see:* **www.visitswansea-bay.com** *. Note: No dogs on Aberavon Sands between 1 May and 30 September*

Don't miss: Swansea's museums and galleries | **Tennant Canal** – built to promote the Swansea docks | **Brunel Tower** – surviving relic of Brunel's revolutionary floating dock

▲ *Swansea Marina from the air*

Swansea

Settled by Vikings and then Normans, Swansea developed on the back of shipbuilding and coastal trade before local coal and West Country ore spawned a burgeoning copper industry. Yet even then, the coast remained largely rural and briefly courted ambitions as a holiday spa. But abundant coal drove the 19th-century steam age and the construction of canals, railways, vast docks and warehousing made the port a gateway to Empire. Iron, steel and tinplate industries boomed alongside copper, zinc and pottery production, drawing workers from across the country and Ireland in a population explosion.

The 20th century brought more change with new docks to receive Persian oil and the construction of the UK's first refinery at Llandarcy in 1922. The Navy began to shift from coal to oil and industry slowly followed. Despite resurgent booms during two World Wars, Britain's coal industry fell into steady decline and cheaper imports gradually eroded the other heavy industry on which the area relied.

Yet, King's Dock remains a working harbour and regeneration has wrought transformation with the Marina, Maritime Quarter and prestigious SA1 multi-use developments, while mussels are farmed in Queen's Dock, harking back to days when wild oysters were harvested around the bay.

Bold architecture on the Swansea waterfront

Bridge of size?: *Swansea's famous Sail Bridge was opened in 2003*

The route: Swansea to Port Talbot

1 A **footbridge over the River Tawe** overlooking the **Barrage** below the **Swansea Marina** marks the beginning of the final leg of the Wales Coast Path.

Swansea's Marina opened in 1982 as the focus of a new maritime development overlooking South Dock. The Swansea Barrage was completed 10 years later, transforming the lower reach of the river into a lake. Lock gates allow passage for boats to the open sea, with a fish ladder beside it to enable salmon, sea trout and eels to migrate to their spawning grounds upriver. Local seals have learnt that this is a good hunting spot for fish, so keep your eyes open.

Turn up the eastern bank beside the river, but after 100 metres, swing right beside a **car park**. Cross **King's Road** and walk through to the **Prince of Wales Dock,** now overlooked by bright new developments. Follow the **quayside** left, turning the corner of the dock basin behind the striking, white-painted building of a former **Norwegian mission church**, another reminder of Swansea's rich maritime heritage.

Some 150 metres beyond a Beefeater restaurant and Premier Inn, a path leads out left to a service road. Go right and then first left beside the **Village**

Urban Resort car park to meet a shared foot and cycleway, **National Cycle Route 4**. Follow it away to the right.

The designated Coast Path intermittently accompanies NCR4 all the way to Margam: watch for signs and cycle symbols on the ground and be aware that cyclists may approach from behind.

After crossing the parallel busway, the track follows it over **Sidings Bridge**, an iconic structure skewed across **Fabian Way**.

Norwegian tin church

There was once a strong link between South Wales and Norway. Scandinavian forests provided pit props for the mines while returning ships took back cargoes of Welsh coal. Built originally beside Newport Docks, the mission served Norwegian sailors in a foreign land. The building was relocated to Swansea's North Dock in 1910 but when the area was redeveloped in 2004, the by then listed building was moved once more to enjoy a new life as a gallery beside the Prince of Wales Dock.

Beyond the **Fabian Way Park and Ride** car park, the path emerges onto a street at **Port Tennant**.

2 Go right, over a crossroad and on past the end of a newer housing development. Forking right across a bridge spanning a remnant of the 👁 **Tennant Canal**, the way degrades to a track past a large building, originally built as a sports centre.

The first canal across Crymlyn Bog was dug in 1788 to take coal from Glan-y-wern pit out to the River Neath. But the Neath was less suited to receive shipping than the Tawe, and in 1817, George Tennant, a London businessman, took over the canal and cut a line through to Swansea. He also contemplated building lock accesses to the river by Briton Ferry, so that traffic could cross from the Neath Canal to his own. However, rather than have barges make a potentially hazardous crossing of a tidal river, he decided the better option was to take his own canal up the west side of the Neath valley and connect the two canals at Aberdulais.

The Tennant Canal finally opened in 1824, running for 8½ miles with only a single lock linking it to the Neath Canal and serving several works and collieries. The canal originally terminated through a sea lock into Fabian Bay, where Tennant built loading wharves and called it Port Tennant. The subsequent construction of the Prince of Wales and King's docks necessitated a short extension and the canal continued in operation into the mid 1930s.

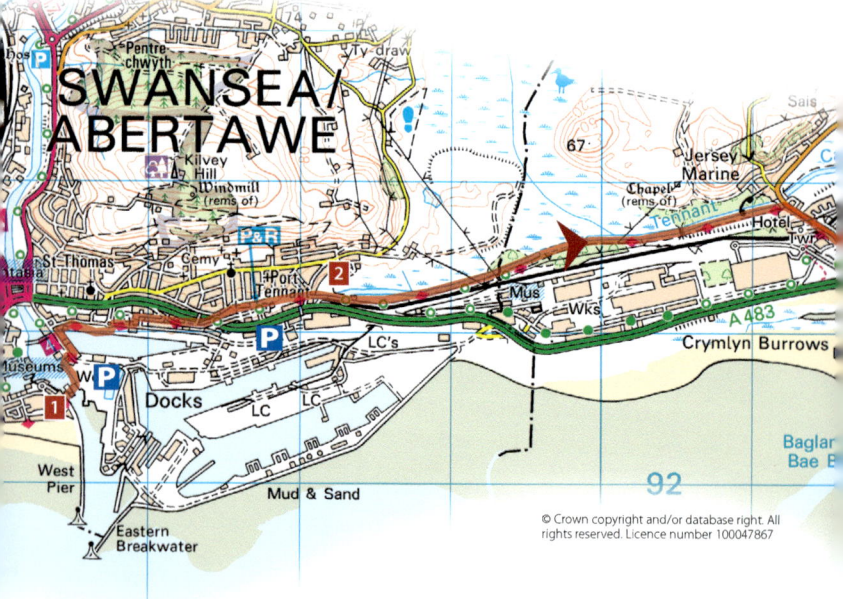

Swans, see?: *The Wales Coast Path follows the Tennant Canal out of Swansea*

Beyond **playing fields**, the track soon passes into wetland wood beside the course of the **disused canal**. At first, the canal is all but lost in reed beds and scrub at the edge of **Crymlyn Bog**, but clear water flowing from the wilderness expanse to the north along the old **Glan-y-wern branch** later brings it to life.

The largest area of fenland in Wales, Crymlyn Bog was almost lost to pollution emanating from the Llandarcy refinery, landfill dumping and the encroachment of development. Its saviour was Andrew Lees, subsequently Campaigns Director for Friends of the Earth, who fought for its preservation. His memorial carries a quotation 'At some point I had to stand up and be counted. Who speaks for the butterflies?' The area is now protected as a National Nature Reserve, Special Area of Conservation (SAC), RAMSAR site and SSSI, featuring the rare Fen Raft Spider.

Further on, an **old concrete bridge** once carried a pipeline linking the former Llandarcy oil refinery to Swansea's docks.

Britain's first crude oil refinery began production in 1922, serviced by a pipeline linking it to the then newly opened Queen's Dock at Swansea. Over time, however, the dock was unable to accommodate ever-larger tankers and in 1961, a new deep-water terminal was built at Angle in Milford Haven, Pembrokeshire. For over 20 years, the oil was pumped across country to the refinery through an 80-mile pipeline. But in 1985, responding to the ever-changing vagaries of oil economics, the refinery was restructured to produce specialist oils rather than fuel and the Milford Haven facility and connecting pipeline closed. The refinery itself finally shut in 1998, the site now being the subject of ongoing redevelopment as a new urban village, Coed Darcy.

Approaching the next bridge at **Jersey Marine**, climb from the canal bank onto the road. Follow it right past the **Towers Hotel** and across a railway to a large roundabout junction with the **A483**.

Jersey Marine is named for the Earls of Jersey, who acquired the estate in the 18th century. Later, there were Victorian hopes of transforming the place into a holiday resort. Yet the dream remained elusive as much of the adjacent coast was subsequently lost to industry. However, a short stretch of

Bog standard: *Crymlyn Bog is the largest area of fenland in Wales and a National Nature Reserve*

unspoiled beach remains beyond the SSSI dunes of Crymlyn Burrows, which can be accessed along a track from the main road opposite the roundabout.

3 Cross left with the shared foot and cycleway and continue beside the main road in the direction of Neath. After ¾ mile/1.2 kilometres, wind beneath an underpass to continue on the other side of the carriageway. Ignore the Earlswood road and walk on **beneath the motorway** up to a major junction. Go right with the **A48** over bridges spanning the Neath valley to a roundabout at **Briton Ferry**.

There is a choice of onward routes to Port Talbot. In the spirit of hugging the periphery of Wales, the official route of the Wales Coast Path seizes the opportunity to head for the coast, running through dunes and along the lovely 3 mile/5 kilometre stretch of **Aberavon Sands** before turning up beside the River Afan into Port Talbot. Despite the proximity of industry, the expanse of Aberavon Sands' unspoiled beach has a fine outlook across the bay and is a great place for collecting shells, paddling in the tide, flying a kite or kite surfing.

The alternative takes to the wooded hills above Baglan and offers a detached perspective of the industrial and suburban coastal strip, which was developed upon the original sea-washed marsh. Its slightly shorter distance tempers the path's ups and downs.

More than meets the eye: *Tidal marshes are often rich with wildlife*

Official route: *Briton Ferry and Port Talbot*

4 Walking anticlockwise against the traffic flow around the roundabout, take the first exit, **Brunel Way**. Follow it over a railway bridge, past a junction and beneath the motorway, shortly reaching the 👁 **Brunel Tower**.

Although long since replaced by a bridge, Briton's ferry across the Neath dates back to the Roman incursion into Wales, when, drawn by the riches of metal ore, invasion forces pushed a military road, the Via Julia Maritima, *along the south coast from Gloucester to Carmarthen. Like Swansea, the estuary offered a landing for centuries, but tidal wharves could not cope with the large ships of the industrial age and in the middle of the 19th century, work began on a floating dock to service the growing steel, tinplate and alloy industries. Its inner and outer basins were separated by a massive floating lock gate designed by Brunel.*

After the Second World War trade through the docks declined and instead many redundant warships were brought here for breaking. The docks finally closed in 1959 and the wet or floating dock was partially filled in, although there is hope that one day the Brunel Dock may be restored.

Just beyond, by a **soaring sculpture**, bear right to skirt **The Quays**, a light industrial development. Over to the right, a muddy tidal reach was once the entrance to **Brunel's floating dock**. After crossing **Baglan Brook** the path skirts industrial compounds, swinging left at the corner of a fence around a **marshy inlet**. At the end, turn right but, where the track later approaches a gate, bear off to walk forward beneath a **pipeline gantry**.

Established by BP in 1963, the industrial site to the left produced petrochemicals until its closure in 2004. The area may be developed in the future.

After passing beneath a pipeline, bear left to continue past **dunes** around the perimeter of a former chemical plant. At the next corner, keep forward through the sand hills to the **foreshore**.

Aberavon Sands *stretch ahead for a good 2 miles, offering the first chance on this final leg of the Wales Coast Path to stride away at the tide line where the waves wash up masses of shells: look out for oysters, razors, cockles and scallops. For the moment, industry, commerce and urbanisation are hidden behind the dunes and the view is across the empty sweep of Swansea Bay back to Mumbles Head, less than seven miles away.*

5 Swing left along the beach. If the tide is out, you can stay with the beach all the way to the stone breakwater of **Jersey Quay**. However at high water, the tide washes the promenade wall and you will need to leave the beach towards the end of the dunes.

If the tide is in, look for a Coast Path waypost, about ¼ mile/400 metres before the start of the sea-front buildings, which marks a path through the sand hills onto the end of the promenade.

About halfway along the **promenade**, a slipway drops onto the beach from the **Coastguard and Inshore Rescue Boat station**s. Close by are a couple of hotels. A little further along the promenade park, opposite a fast food outlet, stands a **sculpture** inspired by a kite tail, which symbolises one of the time-honoured pastimes practised on this superb stretch of open sand.

A huge variety of seashells can be found on Aberavon Sands

Sandy shore: *Backed by dunes, Aberavon Sands stretch for more than three miles*

6 If you've not already done so, leave the sands when you reach the **Jersey Quay breakwater**. *It was built to protect the mouth of the River Afan and the entrance to Port Talbot's docks.* Walk out through a small car park to pick up a footpath beside the entrance, which runs on atop the **sea wall** above the shore. Soon turned inland by the **River Afan**, it heads upstream, eventually emerging onto a street corner by a bridge that once carried the main road into the docks. The bridge is due to be demolished and the route now turns left a little further on into Newbridge Road. Continue ahead past side streets to traffic lights and turn right along Victoria Road with its local shops and supermarket. Cross the dual carriageway on the footbridge and follow the pavement back towards the river. Cross over the signalled pedestrian crossing before continuing to the roundabout at the end of the Port Talbot dockland bypass at **7**.

The onward **official route** to Porthcawl follows the **NCR4** beside the **A4241** to the right, bypassing Port Talbot town centre and continuing through the back streets of **Margam** to a roundabout near **Margam Abbey**. But, on suburban pavement all the way, it offers little of interest and a more appealing option is to continue into town along the link path to join the alternative upland route across the flank of Mynydd Brombil. Both routes are described in the next chapter.

Port Talbot town centre link

7 *To reach the* **town centre***, circle the roundabout anti-clockwise, crossing the* **A4241** *(using the nearby bridge if traffic is heavy) and then a side road before swinging off along a* **cyclepath***. It runs beside the* **River Afan** *to an under-*

Seaside sculpture

Dominating the southern end of the promenade is 'Kitetail'. The largest single piece of street sculpture in Wales, it was inspired by the swirling streamers attached to the kites often flown above Aberavon's expansive beach, while its realisation in steel echoes the town's long association with the industry. Its companion piece, 'Taper' stands nearby and was designed by the same artist, Andrew Rowe

Paragliders often traverse the Aberavon dunes

Aberavon

Sandy paradise in an urban setting

Now subsumed within Port Talbot, Aberavon was a historic settlement beside the river mouth. Though taken by the Normans, the area uniquely continued under the Welsh rule of the Lords of Afan for more than 250 years. A market town developed below the castle and the river mouth was a landing for Margam Abbey. Trade increased during the 18th century, with a network of tramways reaching out to the nearby coal mines and iron and copper smelting works.

At one time, the whole 3-mile run of the sands was backed by dunes. The sands became a popular Edwardian seaside resort for the working families of the industrial valleys. Things changed in the 1950s, with the expansion of the steelworks at Margam. Much of the Aberavon dune system disappeared under a vast new housing development to accommodate the huge influx of workers, the natural sea defences replaced by a 1½-mile promenade. More recent regeneration has created a pleasant promenade and the long strand has gained 'Blue Flag' status. It remains a superb beach and its uninterrupted flat expanse makes it ideal for kite flying and paragliding.

More information: Popular year-round beach for families, bathers and surfers: www.aberavon-beach.co.uk/

Summer in the city: *Lush growth counterpoints the reminders of industry*

pass. Emerging beyond, turn left to cross the river. Swing right beneath another **underpass** *and immediately go left around beside the* **bus station**. *Cross the vehicle entrance and keep ahead past the shelter to a bridge beneath the railway. Emerging beyond, wind back up right beside a short service road. Keep ahead at the top to re-cross the river and then double back left to a riverside path signed to the railway station and shopping area. Ignore the next bridge and continue to a second one in front of Tesco. Over that, bear right towards the* **Civic Centre**. *Keep right past the car park and walk up to the main road. Go right, crossing at the lights to reach a roundabout by a* **Tesco filling station**, *Waypoint* (**10**).

Alternative route: *Briton Ferry to Port Talbot*

The alternative route is waymarked with red rather than blue-backed roundels.

4 Walking anticlockwise around the **A48 roundabout**, cross **Brunel Way** (be careful of fast-moving traffic) to a **footbridge** spanning the roundabout. Cross to the far side and descend the steps on the right. Follow **Old Road** gently uphill past the entrance to McDonald's. After ¼ mile/400 metres, bear left along **Penrhiwgoch**. As that then bends left, keep ahead on a narrow path between a house garage and small substation to rise into **Briton Ferry Wood**. Carry on as a path joins from the left to reach a fork, there taking the left, higher branch. Meeting a

Natural high: *An alternative path high above the coast's busy commerce*

track, go right, gently descending through the trees to another fork. Stay ahead with the main track, soon emerging onto **Thorney Road**.

Go left and immediately bear left up a steep, narrow lane. At a sharp bend, swing off left in front of **Baglan Villa** and then right on a path beside the house rising into the woods. Eventually meeting a path from the left, follow it down right to come out onto a street, **Baglan Heights**. Go right to a T-junction then left along **Darren Wen.** After 75 metres, turn right on a contained path beside a **school playing field** to drop out onto **Ascot Drive**. Go left and then left again at the end past the school entrance. Swing right down the hill and right again at the end.

The figure of St Baglan emerges from the haze of time as a legendary figure, one of nine sons born to by a 6th-century Breton prince, all of whom fled to Britain with St Cadfan to escape the invasion of the Franks. Baglan joined the monastery at Llantwit Major, where St Illtud recognised him as one of God's chosen. He gave Baglan a bishop's crook and sent him off along the coast as a missionary, instructing him to seek out a tree bearing three different fruits and there establish a church.

The crook eventually led him to a spot on the hillside above the mouth of the Neath valley, where he spotted an oak. At its foot a sow and piglets were snuffling amongst the leaves for acorns, bees came and went through a hole in the trunk and in the branches above, birds had built a nest. He deemed this to be the tree for which he searched, but preferred a spot down by the shore for his church. Gathering stones, he began erecting the walls, but each night as he slept the tide washed away the labours of the day. Eventually persuaded that his actions were futile, he returned to the tree, where his efforts then began to bear fruit. The original church was rebuilt during the Middle Ages, but that burnt down in 1954 and remains a ruin.

8 After 100 metres, turn off sharp left along **Bwlch Road**. The narrow, leafy lane climbs out of **Cwm Baglan**, shortly reaching a sharp left-hand bend by a **farm**. Leave through a gate ahead, from which a track runs on past farm sheds and the **ruin of the old Tudor farmhouse**. Soon passing another large building, the way swings right and climbs towards **Mynydd Forest**, the view now opening spectacularly across the coastal plain and Swansea Bay. After ½ mile/800 metres, at a junction, go sharp left and then first right. Carry on across the rising hillside, eventually reaching a gate at the top.

A walker enjoys the view from a gate overlooking the distant coast

Looking down Cwmafan to the coast

Cwm Afan

From iron and industry to quiet countryside

Margam Abbey was smelting iron in Cwm Afan as early as the 13th century using locally mined ore. The industry continued on a small scale, always limited by the amount of charcoal that could be produced from the surrounding woodland. In 1717, the Rice Mansels opened a works at Cwmafan, initially forging local iron, but later smelting ore too.

Coal mining followed in mid-century, producing coke that replaced charcoal as the fuel in the smelting hearths. The early 19th century saw the construction of the first blast furnace. Flourishing industrialisation prompted the construction of Port Talbot Docks in 1837 to replace the tiny harbour of Aberavon. Iron production immediately increased on the back of imports of high quality foreign ore. The industries prospered, eventually employing some 3,000 people.

However, the later part of the century saw a decline as demand shifted away from wrought iron towards steel. Transport costs shifted the geographical advantage away from Cwmafan to the coast.

Today, with the mines and industry gone, the valley has reverted to relative silence and salmon and trout can be found in the river once more.

Down town: *Dropping down from Mynydd Dinas*

The area was inhabited long before the Romans arrived and there is evidence of both Bronze and Iron Age settlements on these hills. Iron Age settlements are generally surrounded by banks and ditches and are commonly referred to as 'forts'. However not all occupy the best defensible position and are better regarded as protected settlement sites rather than purely military ones. The area here was well bestowed with resources, the hill slopes provided grazing and areas for cultivation while the coastal marshes teemed with wildfowl and fish.

Instead of passing through, take a narrow path on the right that runs beside an old boundary thick with bilberry, heather, gorse and broom, high across the flank of **Mynydd Dinas**. Eventually, the way falls to the head of a **stepped path**.

9 Follow it straight down the steep hillside, ignoring a couple of crossing paths and ultimately emerging by cottages onto the end of a lane. Continue down to a T-junction and cross to the path opposite, which drops abruptly beneath the **motorway** to emerge opposite a **roundabout**. Turn left along the **B4286** towards Velindre, walking past the **Civic Centre** and **Princess Royal Theatre**. Ignore the road off left to Cwmafan and cross the **River Afan** to the next roundabout by a Tesco filling station at Waypoint (**10**).

SECTION TWO

Port Talbot to Porthcawl

Distance: *11½ miles / 18.5 kilometres (Alternative - 14 miles/22.5 kilometres)*
Start: *A4241 roundabout SS 759 896 (alternative —Tesco roundabout SS 766 902)*
Finish: *Porthcawl Point SS 818 765* | **Maps:** *OS Landranger 170 Vale of Glamorgan or OS Explorers 165 Swansea and 151 Cardiff & Bridgend*

Outline: Urban roads can be avoided by taking to the hills, subsequently winding back to the coast for a fine walk by the beach to Porthcawl.

Port Talbot's docks and the sprawling Margam steelworks prevent access to the coast, but the upland alternative across the flanks of Mynydd Emroch and Ergyd Isaf is an enjoyable diversion. Crossing Margam Moors gives a taste of what the coastal marshes might have been like before the industrial age. Back with the coast, there's a chance to stride out along the beach to Porthcawl.

Services: *Buses link Port Talbot, Margam and Porthcawl, and Port Talbot has a railway station. There are shops and other facilities in the towns at both ends of the leg, but midway, the only option is at Margam Country Park, a good mile from the path. You'll find hotels by the route at both Port Talbot and Porthcawl. Bridgend Tourism 01656 815332 | tourism@bridgend.gov.*

Don't miss: Margam Stones Museum – one of the most important collections of Celtic crosses in Britain | **Margam Country Park** - Tudor Gothic mansion set in 3.4 km² of glorious parkland | **Kenfig National Nature Reserve** – Special Area of Conservation and SSSI dune and marsh habitat

▲ *Port Talbot steelworks seen across Margam Sands*

Port Talbot

Christopher Rice Mansel Talbot's succession to the family estate in 1824 turned a page in Aberavon's history, transforming the small harbour into a major industrial port. He invested, not only in the coal and iron industries, but also in the infrastructure on which they relied, pioneering railways and establishing the first major floating dock in South Wales.

The Talbot Ironworks began production in 1831 with the docks opening six years later and taking the name of Port Talbot. Expansion continued after his death and the port rivalled both Swansea and Cardiff, its trade reaching a peak in 1923 with the export of three million tons of coal.

Half a century later it was the massive growth of steel that prompted further investment, since the Victorian docks were unable to accommodate ever-larger freighters bringing in ore. Work began on a deepwater tidal harbour, with encircling breakwaters to accommodate massive bulk cargo ships. Full circle came when the old docks reopened in 1998 to berth smaller shipping handling general cargo and the growing trade of biomass fuel imports. And, despite the present uncertainties of the steel industry, the port remains a vibrant element of the economy.

Wales Coast Path signpost on Margam Sands

Official route: **Port Talbot to Margam Roundabout**

The official route out of Port Talbot has little to commend it other than being a good 2 miles/3.2 kilometres shorter than the alternative. However, it may offer a preferable route in poor weather.

1 For the **official route**, follow the roundabout anticlockwise against the traffic flow, leaving first right along a shared foot and cycleway beside the A4241, on **Harbour Way**.

Opened at the end of 2013, the new road bypasses the communities of Taibach and Margam to serve the Margam steelworks complex and the new industry springing up around the regenerated dockland.

Go straight over the next roundabout and immediately cross to continue beside the opposite carriageway. Keep ahead at the next two roundabouts. After a further 350 metres, at a waymark, turn off left to meet a service road.

2 Cross the road and follow the raised path beneath a railway bridge. Emerging beyond, turn sharp right along a track that leads to a car park behind

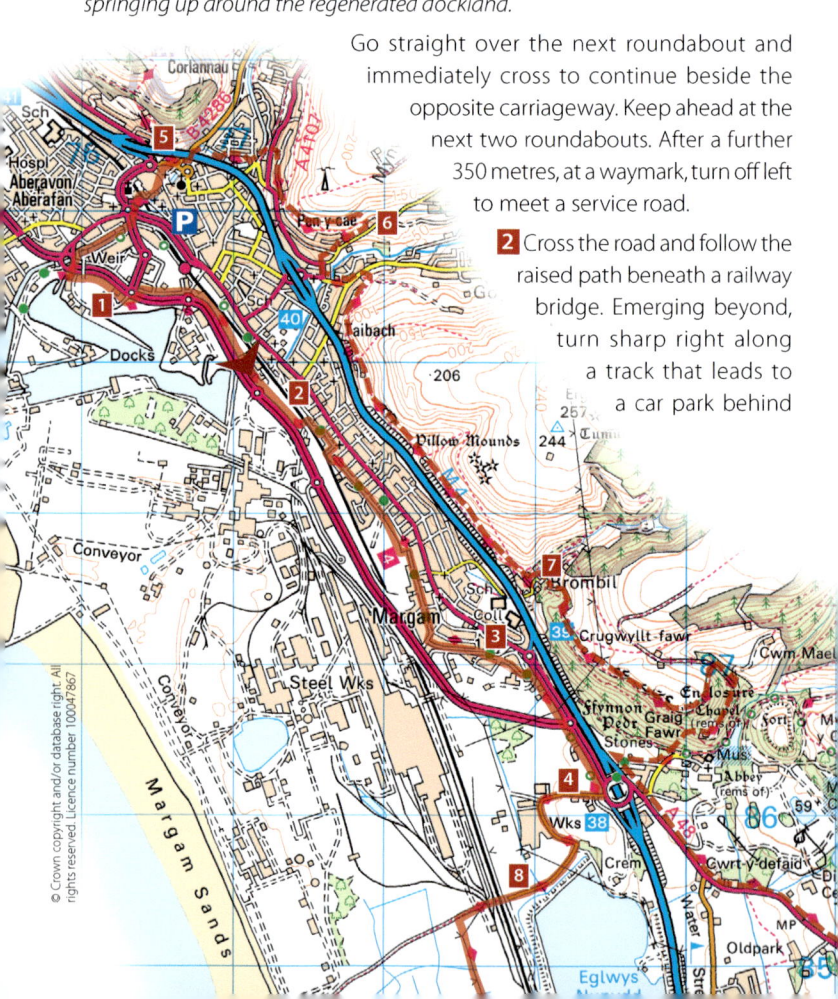

View from the hills: *Looking down to Port Talbot Docks from near Cwm Dyffryn*

Taibach Community Centre. Exit through an opening in the lefthand railings and turn right along a back street. At the end, swing right back to the railway and then left to come out by garages. Wind left and then right along **Prince Street**. Keep ahead as it finishes, the way degrading to a track beside a high-fenced recreation field. The track eventually bends left onto another street. Follow it away right, eventually reaching a skewed T-junction at the very end. Go right and then first left into **Brynhyfryd Road**.

3 After ¼ mile/400 metres, opposite **Cefn Ffynnon**, pass through a gap in the righthand hedge. Cross the main road at pedestrian traffic lights and take the short path opposite onto **Abbots Close**. Go left, but then keep right at a fork, the street shortly curving to a T-junction. Turn right, but as the street then bends sharply right, pass out left to a footway beside the **A48**. Head away to the right, shortly reaching a large **roundabout**. Navigate it anti-clockwise and continue with the main road to the next roundabout above the **motorway** near **Margam Abbey and Country Park**, there meeting the alternative high-level route at **4** (*see page 87*).

Like many of Britain's motorways and main trunk routes, the idea for a strategic road — now the M4 motorway — linking London with South Wales was conceived before the Second World War. Work eventually began on the English section in 1960 with the section into Wales across the River Severn from east of Bristol to west of Newport opening in 1966. A six-mile isolated section bypassing Port Talbot opened the same year and was originally designated A48(M). The M4 eventually reached its present termination in Carmarthenshire at Pont Abraham in 1993, the final section to be completed being the high bridge over the River Neath at Briton Ferry passed in the previous stage of the walk.

Alternative route: *Port Talbot to Margam Roundabout*

Unless you have a compelling reason for following the official route, you should take to the hills behind the town. If you have arrived in Port Talbot via Aberavon Sands (**1**), you must follow the link described in the previous chapter into the town centre and pick up the upland alternative at the roundabout by the **Tesco filling station** at **5**.

The alternative route is waymarked with red rather than blue-backed roundels.

5 Leave the town centre roundabout along a riverside path behind the **Tesco filling station**. After passing beneath the **M4 motorway**, the waymarked route swings right behind a day centre. Although you can cross the river at that point, the official route ignores the bridge and continues beside the car park. At the end, swing right and then left beneath the umbrella of the motorway. After 30 metres, turn left over a bridge and continue right along a back street above the opposite river bank. Emerging onto a street by a **school**, walk forward then turn right, over a bridge, and back across the river to a mini-roundabout.

Go briefly left along **Ynys-Y-Gored**, crossing to a stepped path that leaves on the right. Emerging onto the **A4107** by a **Welsh chapel**, cross over to another stepped path and climb to the top road, **The Uplands**. To the right, it leads back down towards the main road. However, just before the junction, leave through a gate on the left along a rising grass track.

Beyond trees, occasional steep pulls take the way across open hillside along **Pen-y-cae** before the path levels. Carry on until the waymark points right, down the hill, to **Broomhill**. On Broomhill, bear right then left to head down the road.

The fast flowing stream of Ffrwd Wyllt powered corn and fulling mills during the medieval period, but like Cwm Afan, Cwm Dyffryn was overtaken by the Industrial Revolution. During the late 19th century, a railway

High and dry: *A broad grassy path undulates across the lower slopes above Port Talbot*

ran through to Maesteg carrying coal, and there were copper works at the foot of the valley. Opened around 1780, they operated for some 120 years, producing among other things drums used for printing patterned cotton fabric in the Lancashire mills. In the middle of the 19th century, they also produced coinage for the Malay States.

6 Follow the street downhill to the main road and go left to a roundabout. Turn left along **Tan-Y-Groes Place** and then left again at the end along **Dyffryn Road**. After 100 metres, watch for a footpath leaving on the right. Doubling back, climb to a gate ahead. Continue along a contained path, through gates, before breaking out onto the open hillside. Ignoring descending forks, keep to the higher path to contour across the gorse-covered hillside. After crossing a **small bridge** at the foot of **Cwm y Geifr**, the path carries on and later goes through a gate. Eventually meeting the bend of a track, follow it down to **Brombil Farm**. Through a gate, walk forward beside a large shed to a gate from which a path leads out to a lane.

The present farm dates from the 17th century, working land that formed one of the old granges of Margam Abbey.

7 Go left to the end and over a bridge, then left again before swinging sharp right around **Brombil Cottages**. Just beyond, turn off left

Green lung: *Margam Castle, Abbey and Country Park provide a popular green space*

over a stream and follow a rising path into woodland. Over a bridge the path climbs steeply through the trees. At the top, ignore a stile and take the right fork to follow a superb, wildflower-rich path that undulates above a steep, wooded bank. Partway along, the derelict, mast-topped concrete bunkers of a **Second World War radar station** occupy a commanding position above the coastal plain.

Farther on, a craggy outcrop provides another excuse to loiter, the view overlooking a ring of Gorsedd Stones far below that were erected to commemorate the 2003 Urdd National Eisteddfod at Margam. Arranged in a circle, each outer stone represents a Welsh county while the slab at the centre is a ceremonial platform known as the Logan Stone.

Nearby is the site of an Iron Age settlement, its name, **Half Moon Camp** *referring to the crescent-shaped embankments that overlook the foot of the valley below. The prominence served as a lookout during the Napoleonic Wars of the early 19th century from which the local militia could watch for French ships entering the Bristol Channel.*

Beyond, the path steepens downhill beside a wood, emerging onto a lane at the bottom. Go right, walking down to a track emerging on the right.

*A short distance along the track to the left, just before reaching a bridge, look for a well-preserved stone building tucked below the track on the right. Called the **Abbot's Bathhouse**, it's a long, corbel-roofed building with a couple of small windows that dates from around the 14th century. Entered by a door at the southern end, it houses a sunken tank fed by a spring, with steps descending to the water. It was originally a medicinal holy well known as Ffynnon Gyffyr.*

Return to the track and go through a barrier and along a broad woodland path, before bearing right through **Craig y Capel**. There are glimpses across the valley to Margam Castle before the path reaches the ruin of **Capel Mair ar y Bryn** (the chapel of St Mary on the hill).

St Mary's chapel was built in 1470 and is thought either to have functioned as a satellite chapel for use by monks working on the hillside to avoid them having to return to the abbey for prayers or perhaps to serve the local lay community.

Beyond, the way drops steeply into the trees. Meeting a crossing path, go right and then immediately left to emerge onto a junction of lanes at the bottom.

Detour: *To the Margam Stones Museum*
To reach the 👁 **Margam Stones Museum**, walk left along the lower lane.

The ruined Capel Mair ar y Bryn (chapel of St Mary on the hill) above Margam Castle

Port Talbot steelworks

Port Talbot steel industry

Once the largest steel producer in Europe

The Port Talbot steelworks opened in 1901. Serviced by rail and sea and with ready access to limitless coal supplies, they soon established partnerships with their major customers — first the railway rolling stock manufacturers and then the shipbuilders. During the First World War, the business expanded and a second plant was opened on adjacent land at Margam.

Peace saw a much-reduced demand for heavy steel. But Port Talbot and Margam were well-placed once again as Britain began to re-arm with the rise of Nazism in the 1930s.

Further investment after the Second World War centred on the construction of a massive strip mill on the site, which opened in 1951. Within ten years, the complex had become the largest steelworks in Europe and, at its peak, employed 18,000 people.

After nationalisation in 1967 and subsequent re-privatisation 21 years later, the company became part of Corus and has since been taken over by the Tata group, headquartered in India. Today, although the future of Britain's steel industry is in doubt, the plant is capable of producing 4 million tonnes of steel a year.

The onward route, however, is to the right, forking right again in front of a small green. At the lane's end a path swings left, climbing to a large roundabout junction above the motorway (J38, M4). Following the marked **cyclepath**, cross the motorway slip road. Walk against the traffic flow over the bridge and cross the A48 dual carriageway to pick up the lowland route at 4.

Detour: *Margam Abbey, Castle and Country Park*
To reach 👁 **Margam Castle and the Country Park**, follow the A48 towards Pyle. After ¼ mile/400 metres, turn off along the entrance drive, which winds on for a further ½ mile/800 metres to the castle.

Official route: *Margam Roundabout to Sker Point*
4 Back on the **official route**, walk towards the roundabout against the traffic flow and take the first road off right past the entrance to **Margam Crematorium**. The road winds on past Western Wood energy plant and a BOC depot before narrowing to a wooded lane below the **Eglwys Nunydd Reservoir**. *Taking its name from an early Cistercian abbey dedicated to St Non the mother of St David, the reservoir was built to supply water to the Margam steelworks. The full extent of the plant can be seen from the hillside above Margam, running south from the docks for over 2½ miles and extending a mile inland across the coastal strip.*

Prior to the expansion of the works, the coastal plain was largely

Raised boardwalks carry walkers across the reedbeds

88 Wales Coast Path: **SOUTH WALES COAST**

Into the dunes: *A footbridge over the winding Afon Cynffig*

unproductive moor, though part of the land was formerly a grange for Margam Abbey and a small section of its medieval wall is still preserved within the steelworks site.

8 After 1 mile/1.6 kilometres, through gates at the end, cross a succession of **level crossings**. *Be careful: trains on the main lines are fast and frequent, while the sidings beyond are busy with shunting locomotives.* Keep ahead over a crossroad (along which wagons travel between the handling yard and the **Tata Steel plant** to the right) before turning off left through a gate onto a **naturalised track**. *Once a railway line, it is now a pleasant wilderness rich in wildflowers with views opening on the right across Margam Moors to the distant dunes.*

After some ½ mile/800 metres, at a waymark, the path moves right to continue through scrub beside a rising **embankment**. Reaching the end (before private land), swing right to a **boardwalk** across a reedy marsh and through a kissing gate. Turn left over a **concrete bridge** and follow the track. It shortly winds right past a junction into scrub woodland and on below grassed dunes near more railway sidings.

Branching right at a fork, the way then narrows to a path joining another **boardwalk through wetland wood**. Beyond, the path slips through a

Kenfig Pool birdwatching hide

Kenfig National Nature Reserve

A lost town, bottomless pool and stunning flowers

The area around Kenfig was settled well before the Romans arrived. Layers of peat uncovered by the tide have revealed human footprints dating back some 4,500 years, while later beds show hoof prints of cattle. In AD 75 the Roman invaders pushed a road, the *Via Julia Maritima* along the coast from their fort at Caerleon. Numerous Roman artefacts have been found around Kenfig and there is speculation of a marching camp located near the later Norman castle.

After the Romans left, the coastal settlements were vulnerable to Norse raiding parties. A memorial to Bodvoc, a local clan leader thought to have been killed during one such raid in the mid-6th century, once stood beside an ancient British track-

Fen orchid in Kenfig dunes

way at the source of the River Kenfig on Mynydd Margam.

The Normans built a castle beside the River Kenfig, then overlooking an estuary at the edge of a coastal marsh, contained by a line of dunes along the seashore. Under the castle's protection, a medieval town grew up and by the 1350s Kenfig was one of the largest towns in the area with a church, town hall and corn mill. But storms and high tides led to the dunes' destabilisation, and sand began to drift across the grazing marshes onto the town. Old Kenfig was gradually abandoned and the settlement moved inland. Now all that remains amongst the dunes are the forlorn, overgrown ruins of the castle keep.

Bittern skulking in the rushes

> "Kenfig is a treasure trove of rare and beautiful plants"
>
> Plantlife UK

Today, the area is a designated National Nature Reserve, centred upon Kenfig Pool. The largest lake in Glamorgan, it was once reputed to be bottomless and the focus of several sinister legends. In fact, it is only 12 feet deep and seems to have been formed by the dunes blocking streams that once escaped to the sea. During the time of Old Kenfig, it was a source of fish and eels and when Thomas Mansel Talbot took over the Margam estate in the 18th century, he had the lake stocked with pike and other fish. Surrounded by reeds and wet woodland, the lake attracts a huge number of migratory birds, particularly during winter. Teal, tufted duck, pochard, whooper and Bewick's swans all put in an appearance. It is also one of the few places in South Wales where you might catch a glimpse of a bittern. In the summer months, look out for Manx shearwaters and long-tailed skuas.

The dunes are noted for their orchids, which include pyramidal, fragrant and bee orchids. It is also about the only spot left in Wales where you might see the rare fen orchid. Other plants to be found are marsh helleborines, twayblades, stinking iris and sea holly, as well as several species of rare fungi.

More information: For more details, see: www.kenfig.org

Wildlife refuge: *The vast expanse of Kenfig Burrows is a National Nature Reserve*

broken fence and continues below a high, grassy hill of sand. Out to the left, the rambling **Kenfig dunes** impart a real sense of remoteness. Reaching a fork keep left beside the fence, soon meeting a crossing track. Turn left to a **footbridge** spanning the meandering **Afon Cynffig**.

9 TThe route continues along a sandy track running beside a fence along the gently undulating coastal dunes for about 2 miles (passing paths off left to the visitor centre). Eventually, a little further on, bear right at a fork to wind towards the shore, passing a couple of large containers housing a **lifeguard station** above **Sker Rocks**. *For those who've walked along the sands, leave the beach as you approach the rocks at Sker Point and climb to rejoin the coast path as it passes the lifeguard station* 10 .

Alternative route: *Margam Roundabout to Sker Point*
On rare occasions after exceptional or prolonged rainfall, the official path across Margam Moors and Kenfig can become flooded. The alternative involves a lengthy detour via Pyle beside the A48. The more direct B4283 is not recommended as it is a busy road, largely devoid of a footway.

This alternative route is waymarked with red rather than blue-backed roundels.

4 If you have followed the **official route** through the streets of **Margam** to the **Margam Roundabout**, use the cycleway crossings to work your way clockwise across the motorway bridge to pick up to the **A48** south east towards Pyle.

Kenfig Burrows

The vast, rolling dune system of Kenfig Burrows is just one of several such features found along the South Wales coast. Climatic deterioration in the Middle Ages led to a period of heightened storms and tides, causing the sea to throw up sand, which was then blown inland. The old village became smothered and was finally abandoned, the small population moving further inland to escape.

Shallow soil: *A network of sandy tracks cross the back of Kenfig Burrows*

Approaching the lane off to Margam Abbey and the Margam Stones museum, cross the main road and continue with the footway on the opposite side. Keep with the A48 for 3 miles/4.8 kilometres, eventually passing beneath a railway bridge on the outskirts of **Pyle**. Carry on past a service station towards **St James' Church**.

13 Immediately before the **churchyard**, turn sharp right along a broad track (not the concrete path) that descends behind houses into trees. At the bottom, cross the **Afon Cynffig** and go right, shortly swinging left to climb beside the railway embankment. After ¼ mile/400 metres, beside a railway crossing, go over a stile on the left and follow a track out to a lane.

Walk right past **Dunraven Stud** down to **Llanmihangel Farm**, there bearing right over a stile beside a gate to a **footbridge spanning the Afon Cynffig**. Follow the sandy track ahead, bearing left past a gate to rise into trees. Over a couple of stiles at the top strike ahead across a sloping field to another gate at the far side. Cross a training track to a stile opposite and follow the ongoing grass path into more trees. Branch right at a fork, shortly emerging by kennels to follow a track out to the **B4283**.

Section 2: **Port Talbot to Porthcawl** 95

14 Go left beneath a railway bridge, leaving sharp right along a track some 50 metres beyond. Through gates, walk beneath the motorway onto the edge of the dunes beyond and swing left on a path parallel to the motorway. Beyond a gate, the way curves gently right towards the tower of **Mawdlam Church**. Emerging onto a road near the **Angel Inn,** follow it right for ½ mile/800 metres, passing the **Prince of Wales** before turning in at the entrance to **Kenfig National Nature Reserve.**

15 Walk through the car park passing right of the **visitor centre** to a fork just behind. Bear right, heading towards **Kenfig Pool**, which you can see ahead. Emerging from between trees, keep ahead across a couple of open areas of grass. Beyond, as a path joins from the right, keep ahead to a fork and bear right. The path continues beyond through shrubby dunes, shortly continuing across a **duckboard**. Further along the way rises along a ridge of dunes between wet areas and shortly encountering the broad crossing track of the official route at **SS 787 808**.

Reed fringed Kenfig Pool is a haven for wildfowl

Days by the sea: *Rest Bay is popular with local families during the summer*

Rejoin the **official route** here and turn left. Continue to **Sker Point**.

As on much of Britain's coast, shipwrecks have been an all too frequent an occurrence at Sker Point. Sometimes 'wreckers' deliberately lured vessels aground to plunder their cargoes, but navigational error and natural disaster were the more usual causes of tragedy.

In December 1753, the captain of the French schooner Le Vainqueur bound for Le Havre from Lisbon, missed the mouth of the English Channel and instead turned into the Bristol Channel, a not uncommon mistake at the time. The ship grounded on the rocks of Sker Point and although eight hands survived, the Captain and Mate were drowned.

A band of villagers descended on the wreck to loot its cargo of fruit and planking before the authorities arrived on the scene. Some 17 men were arrested and one was hanged to underline the severity with which the offence was viewed. But the potential bounty to the poor folk of the coast was great and it was neither the first nor the last ship to suffer such a fate.

10 The ongoing path soon leads through a gate and kissing gate before curving left to a junction. Bear right to remain by the coast above the rocks, a wall shortly shepherding the path towards the sandy beach of **Rest Bay**. Beyond a kissing gate by a second **lifeguard station**, a boardwalk takes the route past the links of the **Royal Porthcawl Golf Club**. Keep going as it eventually gives way to concrete, ultimately turning from the beach onto a drive by the golf club entrance.

11 The path is signed to the right, eventually joining the promenade road into **Porthcawl**. However, you can avoid the tarmac by keeping to the edge of the low cliffs behind Rest Bay across the small nature reserve of **Lock's Common**.

Backing a wild fringe of low limestone cliff, Lock's Common was the original site of the golf club, but the narrow strip by the coast is now a small nature reserve and rich in tiny wildflowers. Amongst those to look out for are lady's bedstraw, betony, rock samphire, tormentil and mouse-ear hawkweed.

Beyond **Hutchwns Point**, there is no alternative but to follow the **Esplanade** to **Porthcawl Point** **12**, where there are plenty of cafés and shops.

Porthcawl promenade seen from the beach

SECTION THREE

Porthcawl to Ogmore

Distance: *9 miles/14.5 kilometres* | **Start:** *Porthcawl Point SS 818 765* | **Finish:** *Ogmore-by Sea car park SS 861 755* | **Maps:** *Ordnance Survey OS Explorer 151 Cardiff & Bridgend and Landranger 170 Vale of Glamorgan*

Outline: Beyond the resort, there is easy walking between dunes and sea along the first stretch of the Glamorgan Heritage Coast.

After skirting Porthcawl's harbour, the route makes a brief detour from the coast at the edge of the town before returning to continue above two popular sandy bays. Beyond Newton Point, the path skirts another, larger bay at the fringe of Merthyr-mawr Warren before being turned by the Ogmore River. Heading inland at the edge of the dune system, it then picks up a quiet lane to the tiny hamlet of Merthyr Mawr before crossing the rivers Ogmore and Ewenny just above their confluence and returning to the sea.

Services: *Porthcawl is served by bus with a full range of services in the main street, only a minute's walk from the route. The town also has several hotels and guest houses. Ogmore-by-Sea has only a small shop cum post office and café bar, but accommodation may be found at nearby Ewenny. There is a pub, The Pelican in her Piety, beside the route at Ogmore Castle*

Don't miss: Merthyr-mawr Warren – second highest dunes in Europe | **Candleston Castle** – 14th-century manorhouse | **Ogmore Castle** – Norman castle ruins on River Ogmore

▲ *Looking back across the Ogmore River to Merthyr Mawr*

Porthcawl

Porthcawl developed during the 19th century to export coal and iron ore brought by tramway from the Llynfi and Garw valleys and the Cefn Cribwr ridge. But the switch to steel and import of foreign ore impacted on local industry and, while coal remained important, the larger ships outgrew the harbour. By 1906, Port Talbot and Barry had taken the trade.

But fine beaches and sheltered bays made Porthcawl an ideal resort and, as early as 1832, the industrial tramway was instead bringing in trippers. With grand sea-front hotels and a promenade to celebrate Victoria's Golden Jubilee in 1887, the 'miner's holiday fortnight' became an annual ritual.

Named after the famous Brooklyn resort, the Coney Beach funfair opened after the First World War, its first ride being a wooden roller coaster that ran for 60 years. Other attractions included roller-skating, a cinema, open-air swimming, boating and a ballroom, while the Grand Pavilion overlooking the Esplanade remains a classic symbol of Porthcawl's heyday.

Today's attractive Harbour Quarter and marina has transformed the original dock and incorporates a rare wharf-side warehouse, a hexagonal cast-iron lighthouse and the last surviving fragment of the Dyffryn, Llynfi and Porthcawl Railway.

Relaxing in the sun on Porthcawl promenade

The route: **Porthcawl to Ogmore-by-Sea**

1 Follow the ongoing road from **Porthcawl Point** as it swings past the marina development on your right. At the top of the harbour, turn right along **Eastern Promenade** above **Sandy Bay**. Approaching the amusement park at the far end of the promenade, when the tide is out, you can leave the road and walk across the head of the beach to the lifeguard station on **Rhych Point**. Otherwise, stay with the road as it turns away to a junction and go right. Keep right at a roundabout and walk for ¼ mille/400 metres to a mini-roundabout. Turn sharp right then take the first left along **Sandy Lane**, which leads back to the coast.

Leaving Porthcawl, the route enters the Glamorgan Heritage Coast, an unbroken 14-mile stretch of unspoiled cliff and shore that includes some of the largest dune systems in northern Europe.

2 The Wales Coast Path is routed left through the dunes to the brightly yellow-painted lifeguard station on the neck of **Rhych Point**, but other than at high tide, you can reach the same point along the beach. Join the

track away from the lifeguard station, forking off beside a caravan site along a raised path that curves around the head of **Trecco Bay** to a car park on **Newton Point**. Despite being one of the largest caravan sites in the country, it is soon passed and again, if the tide is out, you can cut across the beach instead. Follow the promenade road away for 600 metres before turning right into a second car park.

3 The Wales Coast Path continues along a track at the far end through the dunes behind the beach. After 1 mile/1.6 kilometres, reaching a waymark just beyond the tide-washed outcrop of **Black Rocks,** if you have not already done so, head out onto the beach past the **Merthyr-mawr Warren**.

4 Approaching the **Ogmore estuary**, the path turns in by another waymark to follow the river upstream at the edge of the 👁 **Merthyr-mawr National Nature Reserve**.

Merthyr-mawr Warren and Kenfig Burrows were part of a single dune system that once extended all the way to Gower. Most has been lost to the development of towns, docks and sea defences, but what remains suggests a truly impressive natural feature. At over 200 feet, the Merthyr-mawr dunes are the highest in northern Europe and extend over an area of 1¼ square miles (3.2 square kilometres).

There is evidence of human presence from the Mesolithic through to the Iron Age and tools, pottery and burials have been found across the whole area. Like the dunes of Kenfig, climatic change in the 14th century brought a period of abnormally high tides, repeated storms and high rainfall, destabilising the system and causing it to creep inland. Today, the area contains a wonderful diversity of habitats from bare sand and embryonic dunes to natural woodland. The youngest dunes are found by the shore while further inland, they stand on a limestone escarpment and have been colonised by grasses and a range of plants

Dune buggy?: *Merthyr Mawr's dunes are popular for horseriding and support rare insects*

that include local rarities such as rock sea lavender, sea spurge and hutchinsia. There is scrub and woodland too; in the wetter areas you will come across alder and willow, while elsewhere there are birch, sycamore and pine. In all, over 300 species of plant have been recorded. The area is particularly important for the richness of its invertebrate life, with several species of bee and wasp and many butterflies including the rare grizzled skipper. Look out too for the great green bush cricket, the largest in Britain.

The dune system is now largely stable, but this ironically is threatening some aspects of the habitat. Sea buckthorn, planted in the middle of the 19th century to help consolidate the dunes, began to take over, changing the character of large areas to thorny scrub. Much has been removed and in other areas, cattle are used to control its spread. A rejuvenation programme to increase the area of bare sand has also begun which will encourage a cycle of new dune formation, ensuring the continuance of essential habitats for many insects and plants such as petalwort.

The path sweeps in around the head of a marshy apron, finding firmer ground at the foot of the dunes. After ½ mile/800 metres, watch for a post at the edge of the dunes. It directs the route away from the river along the broad, sandy channel of a usually-dry stream bed, a small bridge offering a dry crossing should there be water. The route then heads into woodland, to shortly reach **Candleston car park**, behind which is 👁 **Candleston Castle**.

The Castle is said to take its name from the de Cantilupes, who are believed to have been the first tenants of the manor in the 12th century. The castle, in reality a fortified house, dates from the 14th century, but was in all probability

Orchids at Merthyr-mawr

The Merthyr-mawr dunes are the second highest in Europe. Amongst the many plants to be found there are several species of orchid, which favour the low-lying, wetter areas. Look out for the southern and early marsh orchids, which flower around the beginning of June, or the marsh helleborine, said to be one of Britain's most beautiful species, which follows a short while later.

raised on the site of an earlier building. Although the drifting sands covered its coastal farmlands, the house escaped engulfment by being sited on slightly higher ground. The building has been much altered during the course of its life, even having decorative crenellations added before it was finally abandoned in the 19th century.

5 Leave the car park along a narrow leafy lane, which later opens to fields before reaching the tiny settlement of **Merthyr Mawr**.

Thatched cottages and an ancient-looking church give the hamlet a timeless quality, though in reality the present church dates only from the middle of the 19th century. Dedicated to St Teilo, a 6th-century bishop and supposed cousin of St David, the church may be the latest in a succession that extends back to the 9th century or before. Merthyr Mawr translates as the 'great shrine', suggesting an ancient cemetery of some importance. One of the stones in the small collection protected beneath a porch to the north of the church is a memorial to Paulinus, a 6th-century Roman missionary and first bishop of York. Much later is the 14th-century preaching cross, which stands to the south of the church.

Wales Coast Path waymarker between Newton and Merthyr Mawr Warren

Sands of time: *Ruined Candleston Castle survives on raised ground above the shifting sands*

After skirting St Teilo's extensive **churchyard**, fork right to reach a small car park and **footbridge across the Ogmore River**.

> **Alternative route:** *Low tide stepping stones to Ogmore Castle*
> The ongoing path offers a shortcut leading to **stepping stones** (which can be slippery) across the **Ewenny River**, beyond which, a path climbs beside 👁 **Ogmore Castle** to the B4524 opposite an inn, **The Pelican in her Piety**.
>
> *The unusual name for the pub across the road is an allegorical reference to the sacrificial love and resurrection of Christ. The depiction of a mother pelican plucking at her breast to draw blood to sustain her young was often used as a medieval heraldic device symbolising self-sacrifice; it's actually a misinterpretation of the practice of adult pelicans regurgitating food for their young.*

6 The **official path** leaves over a stile on the left, immediately after the bridge across the **Ogmore River**. Strike out across pasture to a second **footbridge spanning the Ewenny**, a little way upstream of the stepping stones, from which a contained path leads up to the same road.

Dawn's early light: *The rising sun illuminates morning mist near Ogmore Castle*

Detour: *To Ewenny Priory*

Some 1¾ miles/2.8km to the left, just beyond the **village of Ewenny** on the south bank of the Ewenny River is **Ewenny Priory**. Although the priory is now a private residence, the outer walls are impressive and the adjacent church is worth a visit, particularly if you have gone to the village in search of accommodation.

A Benedictine house, Ewenny Priory was founded in 1141 and unusually incorporates impressive defences, the outer walls looking more like a castle than a church. Indeed, the place formed part of the Norman defence of the area against Welsh raiders. Inside the church, massive Norman pillars line the nave and in the south transept are carved stones, including tombs of the priors and of the Carne and Turbevill families, who have held the priory since the Dissolution. Look too for the intricately carved tomb of the priory's founder, Maurice de Londres.

To continue on the **official route**, cross the road and follow the pavement until, just before the pub, the path goes up steps behind the pub and runs across Ogmore Down parallel to the road. Cross the road towards **Portobello House**.

7 The route continues above the river. Approaching the coast, take the higher path above low cliffs, which ultimately leads to a large car park overlooking the estuary, at **8**.

Ogmore Castle

Established in the 12th century by William de Londres, Ogmore Castle, along with nearby Coity and Newcastle castles, asserted Norman superiority in this corner of Wales. Built to guard a ford near the estuary, the castle was soon consolidated in stone by his son Maurice, the founder of Ewenny Priory. The moat filled with the rising tide and his keep is held to be one of the oldest buildings in South Wales.

Ogmore to Llantwit Major

Distance: *10 miles/16 kilometres* | **Start:** *Ogmore car park SS 861 755* | **Finish:** *Col-huw Point car park SS 956 674* | **Maps:** *Ordnance Survey OS Landranger 170 Vale of Glamorgan or OS Explorer 151 Cardiff & Bridgend*

Outline: The next section runs along the top of undulating cliffs, an invigorating walk with impressive views along the coast.

Ahead, the coast gradually rises in striking cliffs, attaining just over 250 feet at its highest point beyond Dunraven Park above Traeth Bach. Below, the receding tide reveals impressive shoals of wave-cut platform and mostly inaccessible beaches; there are only a handful of places where the sea can be safely reached. The path largely follows the undulating rim of the cliffs, periodically dropping to a beachhead or to cross the mouth of a deep cwm.

Services: *There are few facilities on the coast but you'll find toilets by the car parks at Ogmore-by-Sea, Dunraven, Nash Point and Col-huw, and snack cafés at Dunraven, Nash Point and Col-huw. Other facilities necessitate an inland detour; there is a shop and post office, café bar and bus service in the village at Ogmore-by-Sea, with pubs at Southerndown, Monknash (accommodation too) and Marcross. Llantwit Major is served by both bus and rail and has full facilities and shops.*

Don't miss: Glamorgan Heritage Coast – 14 mile unbroken stretch of spectacular limestone cliffs | **Nash Point lighthouses** –19th-century transit lighthouses | **St Donat's Church** – 12th-century church in the shadow of a medieval castle

▲ *Ogmore Castle and the nearby stepping stones from the air*

Ogmore

Winding out to sea through a tidal inlet at the edge of the Merthyr-mawr Warren, the Ogmore River was once one of the finest salmon rivers in South Wales, even its name is said to derive from 'eog' - Welsh for salmon. Pollution during the Industrial Revolution drove the fish away, but the last 30 years have seen them returning to their former breeding grounds.

Apart from a scattering of houses and farms, there was little to Ogmore until the 19th century, indeed the name 'Ogmore-by-Sea' only appeared in the 20th century. The main settlement had been inland, centred upon Sutton quarries, where a fine, white lias limestone had been cut since the Middle Ages. Soft enough to saw when freshly cut, it subsequently hardens with weathering and was reputedly used in the Palace of Westminster. The present village above the coast grew as a resort during the 19th century, at one time supporting three hotels and several cafés and restaurants.

Children playing in Afon Ogmore where it flows across the beach

The route: **Ogmore to Llantwit Major**

1 Skirt the seaward edge of the sprawling car park, leaving through a gate at the southern tip. Continue below a wall along a grassy shelf overlooking the rocky platform backing the beach, a vantage exploited by fishermen when the tide is right. (If you wish to divert into the village, where there is a convenience store, post office and café bar, branch off shortly after the wall ends to pick up a rising path. Cross a lane at the and climb to the top road.)

Carry on towards impressive cliffs that rise ahead. Now the Glamorgan Heritage Coast begins in earnest. After some ½ mile/800 metres, at a waypost, the path curves inland along the base of a shallow gully.

2 Approaching the road, swing sharp right beside a stone wall and head back towards the coast to walk on above the cliffs, *from which there is a fine retrospective view beyond Tusker Rock to Porthcawl and the Gower peninsula*. The path is soon turned inland again by another **gully**, but re-

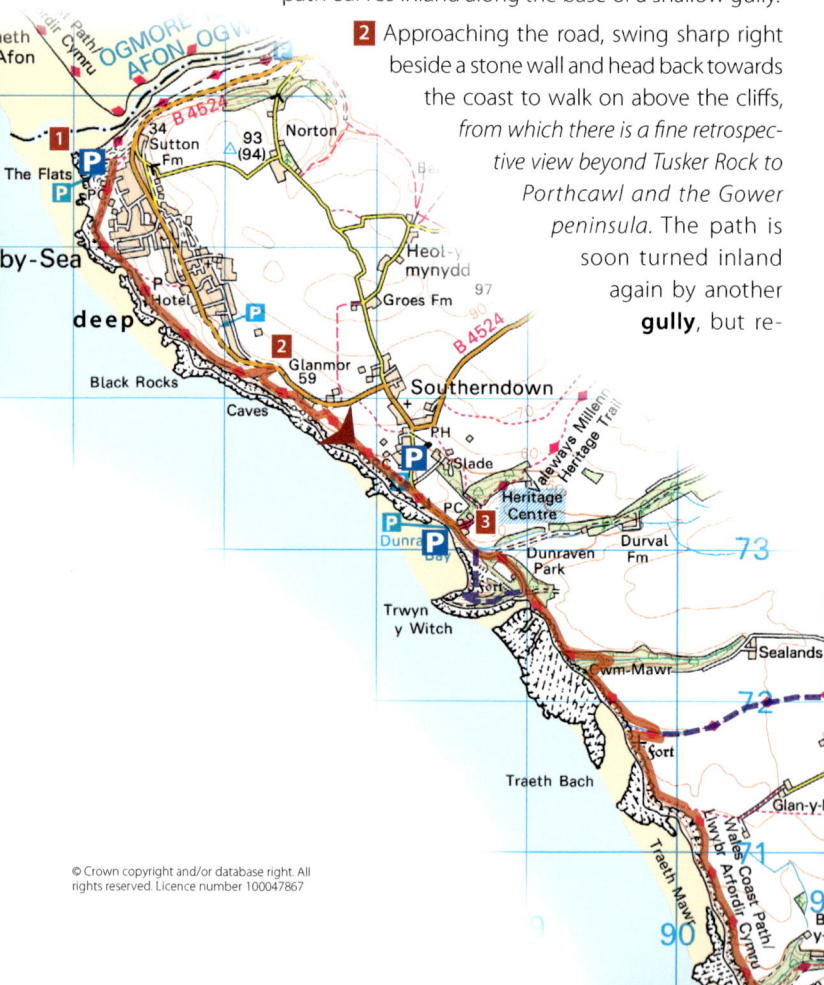

White cliffs: *Walkers backed by distinctive limestone cliffs near Southerndown*

sumes its clifftop course behind **West Farm Barn**. *Seen across the Bristol Channel is the distant Somerset coast, its cliffs rising to the open expanse of Exmoor behind.*

After ½ mile/800 metres, approaching a wall, leave at a kissing gate to pass through a small car park onto the lane. Footpaths on either side accompany the lane down to a car park at **Dunraven Bay**. Walkers are advised to use the path on the left because of unguarded cliffs, but if you venture across for the views, be careful near the edge. The official path continues to a set of steps behind the café.

The **Glamorgan Heritage Coast Centre** *at Dunraven is housed in the estate's former laundry, which is situated just a short distance up the lane behind the beach. There is an information centre, exhibition area and small shop.*

3 The coast path continues at the far side of the car park through the lodge gates into the **Dunraven Estate** and follows a drive rising behind **Trwyn y Witch**.

Detour: *Informal paths lead onto the headland*
Known as Trwyn y Witch, or Witches' Point, the headland enjoys great views and is the site of an Iron Age fort that remained occupied after the Romans' departure at the end of the 4th century. It would have served as a defensible position against coastal raids by Vikings, Irish and Saxons.

Geometrically stacked limestone strata at Nash Point

Glamorgan Heritage Coast

Stunning cliff scenery and 300 million year-old fossils

The cliffs beyond Ogmore-by-Sea display a wonderful mixture of bedded limestones, shale and conglomerate, variously coloured golden to white, grey and blue. The oldest rock lies at the base, a grey Carboniferous limestone that was laid down more than 300 million years ago in a sub tropical sea. It is rich in aquatic fossils such as crinoids, brachiopods and corals.

Succeeding formations were lost to erosion and that now sitting uncomfortably (a geological term referring to missing layers) above the limestone is a coarse conglomerate washed out from a largely desert hinterland. As the earth moved into the Jurassic period around 205 mil-

Ammonite in Carboniferous limestone

lion years ago, the land was again flooded beneath a shallow sea and further alternating layers of shale and limestone were deposited. Fosssils are abundant in these rocks too, with ammonites, brachiopods, gastropods and gryphea of 'Devil's toenails' all fairly common. However, strata laid down since then have again been worn away.

The most recent geological event to affect this coast was the last glacial period, which ended around 10,000 years ago. South Wales lay at the limit of glaciation, a vast tundra stretching to the south where the ground was locked in permafrost. The eventual thaw produced torrential flows of meltwater that gouged out the deep cwms now breaking the coast, which itself was redefined in response to a period of widely fluctuating sea levels.

Rectangular bedded limestone and sea-rounded boulders near Llantwit Major

> *"This is one of the best places in Wales to hunt for Jurassic fossils including giant brachiopods and ichthyosaurus bones"*
>
> www.visitwales.com

Facing the onslaught of Atlantic gales and the second highest tidal range in the world, the cliffs are subject to differential erosion, where removal of the softer, intervening shale layers leads to undercutting and collapse of overlying bands of harder limestone.

The uncultivated fringe of the cliff top supports a wonderful diversity of wildflowers, with rock rose and wild thyme thriving on the nutrient-poor limestone soils, while areas of richer soil and woodland give rise to cowslip, dog violet and bird's foot trefoil. The wind- and salt-blasted cliffs harbour their own plants, including buck's-horn plantain and sea carrot. In places, dense thickets of thorn line the cliff edge, their boughs bent by the relentless battering of the prevailing wind. Frustratingly they sometimes obscure the view, but their roots offer some stability to the ever-crumbling cliff edge.

More information: For more details, see: www.valeofglamorgan.gov.uk

Timeless scene: *A rising tide in Dunraven Bay at dusk*

To continue on the **official route**, ignore the junction to the overflow car park and fork right, following the main drive past **Dunraven's walled garden and ice tower**.

After the Normans settled in the 12th century, William de Londres of Ogmore Castle gave the Dunraven estate (and a knighthood) to his steward Arnold Le Boteler (subsequently anglicised to Butler) as a reward for organising the successful defence of Ogmore during his absence. The medieval house was later transformed into a castellated Victorian mansion overlooking extensive walled gardens.

During two world wars, the house served as a hospital, the family finally leaving in the 1940s. After a brief period as a hostel for the Workers Travel Association it was left empty and finally demolished in 1963. The local council has restored the extensive walled garden, which, together with several nature walks on the estate, is open to the public.

Where the track bends left, bear right up to a historic deer gate and along a waymarked path that runs on above the cliffs, with rewarding views.

After ¼ mile/400 metres, reaching a stone wall, go left to a small gate from which a stepped path drops into the delightful woods of Cwm-Mawr. Over a bridge spanning the stream at the bottom climb right to regain the cliff top. The path dips again a short distance further on, this time into Cwm Bach, with steps on either side of the valley.

At the bottom, if you follow the path right, you will reach the spot where, when the water flows, the stream cascades over the cliff. The onward path however is to the left along the base of the valley to a stile in a crossing wall.

Detour: *To Wick*

With your back to the valley wall, turn left over a stile, where a path leads to the tiny hamlet of Wick — on the Millennium Heritage Trail — where there are two pubs, the **Lamb & Flag** and the **Star Inn**.)

However, to continue on the **official route** along the coast path, bear right at the top of the steps beside the fence, then left at the gap. Follow the field edge back above the valley, passing through another kissing gate to regain the coast. For the next mile/1.6 kilometres, the path undulates along the top of high cliffs, below which the inaccessible, unspoiled expanses of Traeth Bach and Traeth Mawr are revealed at low tide. Nearing **Cwm Nash**, watch for a stile on the right at the start of a fence, over which the path slants down past a curious stone building. Towards the bottom, swing left above another fence to a gate then double back to a bridge spanning **Nash Brook**. You can follow the stream down onto the beach at low tide.

Sweeping layers of limestone on the wave-cut platform on Traeth Mawr

Detour: *To pretty Monknash village*

For an interesting side trip, a path accompanies the stream heading up the valley to **Monknash**, a pretty village surrounded by the ruined buildings of a monastic grange. A satellite to the Cistercian abbey at Neath, it was a sizeable settlement growing grain and other produce for the abbey. The village has accommodation and the **Plough & Harrow,** a pub dating from the 14th century.

4 The onward **official route** tackles a stiff, zigzagging climb up the opposite side of the valley. The effort is rewarded by another easy stretch along airy cliffs, from which there are fine views across the Bristol Channel. Approaching Nash Point, cross a stile to pass through the impressive embankments of another **Iron Age coastal fort**, although again, much of the enclosed settlement site has been lost to erosion. Just beyond the stile, watch for a waypost that marks the path descending left along the base of a fold to a bridge across **Marcross Brook**.

Detour: *Access to the beach*

To the right, a path leads down to the rocky foreshore, which is accessible at low tide.

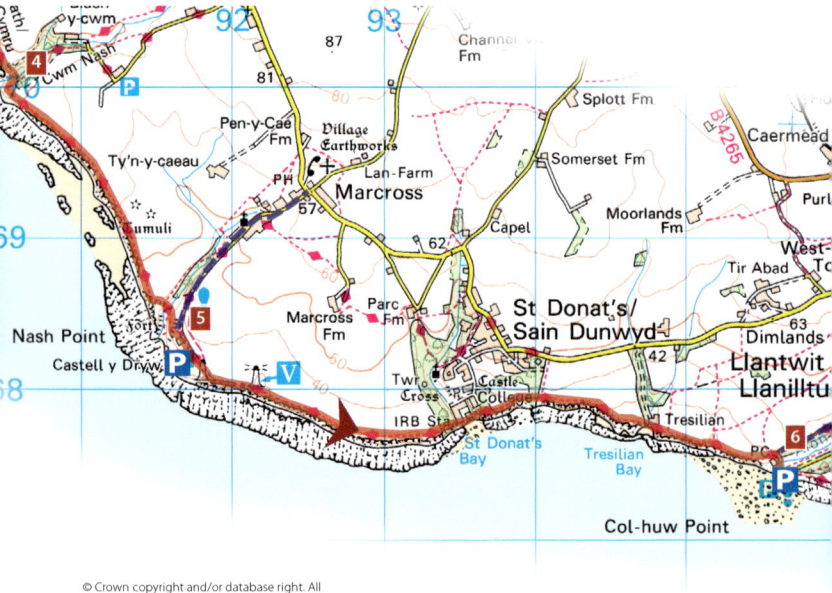

© Crown copyright and/or database right. All rights reserved. Licence number 100047867

Coastal cascade: *Nash Brook tumbles over a final, seaweed encrusted ledge into the sea*

Detour: *To the Horsehoe Inn at Marcross*
The path to the left winds up a pretty wooded cwm to **Marcross**, where there is yet another pub, the **Horseshoe Inn**.

The **official route** continues ahead over the bridge; a short but strenuous pull takes the path up the valley side to a car park, where a small **refreshment cabin** has a reputation for excellent home-made Welsh cakes. Look out, too, for information boards about this unique area.

More than one ship has been involved in multiple disasters in the Bristol Channel, one such being the BP Explorer, a small tanker transporting fuel oil from Swansea up the River Severn to Worcester. On 16 February 1961, having loaded a cargo of petrol, she had passed Avonmouth on the evening tide and was attempting to cross to the deepwater channel on the northern bank by Beachley Point, a spot notorious for strong currents and turbulence. The ship apparently touched bottom during the manoeuvre and capsized in the dark. She was carried on upstream with the tide, striking the Severn Railway Bridge, which had already been damaged during an incident the previous October when two fuel barges struck a pier, bringing down two of the spans. With the changing tide, the drift reversed and dawn eventually broke to find the Explorer's upturned hull beached some 4 miles/6.4 kilometres downstream on Lydney Sands.

Beauty in blue: *Sundown at Nash Point*

The wreck floated back upstream on the next tide, passing the bridge once more and finally grounding off Awre. At first only the captain's body was found, some way downstream at Oldbury-on-Severn, with the other four crew members initially pronounced missing, presumed dead until they too eventually washed ashore.

It took until April to refloat the wreck and tow it to Sharpness, where it was rebuilt. By the end of the year it was back into service as the BP Driver. But disaster struck again on 31 January 1962. While returning empty to Swansea it was caught by a violent squall off Nash Point and driven onto the rocks below the cliffs. Happily the crew managed to clamber ashore, but this time the ship was badly holed and beyond salvage.

5 Follow the drive beyond the car park to the 👁 **Nash Point lighthouses**, passing through a gate into a walled compound. Wind round behind the stubby **tower of the older light**, the **keepers' cottages** and on past a building housing the compressors for the massive foghorns that sit on the roof. Over a stile beyond the **second lighthouse**, the path continues above crumbling cliffs for another ¾ mile/1.2 kilometres. There are some splendid views, but in places, high, wind-sculpted banks of bramble and blackthorn obscure the prospect.

Approaching St Donat's, the path crosses a stile before descending a series of steps through a dense grove of stunted, ivy-clad sycamore. The path emerges onto a broad concrete quay.

Detour: *To St Donats Church*

The path immediately to the left leads out to St Donat's, where you can visit the interesting Norman church.

St Donat's Church

👁 **St Donat's Church** was founded with the castle in the 11th century, shortly after the Normans arrived in Glamorgan. Local legend maintains it was already a Christian site, established by the daughter of Caractacus in the 1st century. Overlooking a sheltered bay, it would have provided a landing for early Christian missionaries. The Norman dedication to St Donat, a patron saint of seafarers replaced that to St Gwerydd, a 5th-century Welsh saint.

The dumpy west tower at Nash Point

Nash Point lighthouses

Twin lights to make a safer coast

With major ports on both sides of the narrowing Bristol Channel, the waters here have always been busy. The second highest tidal range in the world, strong currents and wild weather driven in from the Atlantic exacerbate the problems of shoals and sandbanks beneath the waves. Navigation, particularly in poor visibility has never been easy; indeed, even into the 19th century skippers have mistaken this water for the English Channel. Add to these difficulties engine and other failures and the deliberate actions of Wreckers; it is no wonder that these waters are a graveyard for hundreds of ships, their crews and passengers.

The twin lighthouses at Nash were built in response to the disaster of the paddle steamer *Frolic*, which foundered off the point on Nash

The iconic east lighthouse at Nash Point

Sands in March 1831 with the loss of all 78 passengers and crew. The tragedy spurred the authorities into action and it took just 17 months to design, build and commission the lights. Placed as transit beacons, they enabled ships to navigate up the channel well clear of the dangerous shoal.

Since the 1920s, the light of the lower, western tower has not been used; its lantern and lens being removed in the 1950s. The danger is now indicated by red sector lights — coloured segments within the lens of the eastern light. If the ship is on course, the pilot will see a white light, but if the ship is in the danger zone, the light will show red.

Originally lit by whale oil and then paraffin, the eastern light was converted to electricity in the 1960s and is visible from over 20 miles away. Nash, like all UK lighthouses, is now fully automated and the point's eastern light has the distinction of being the last in Wales to be demanned in 1998. The light itself is opened to visitors on weekend afternoons throughout the summer.

The squat building between the two towers with a large horn on the roof is a foghorn, installed in 1906.

Nash Point's east tower was the last manned lighthouse in Wales

It too has been retired, but is still in working order and sounded twice a month for the benefit of visitors.

The adjacent aerial tower is a DGPS (Differential Global Position System) reference station, which enhances the accuracy of standard GPS by transmitting a correction signal from a known fixed position.

The lighthouses stand within their own SSSI as the rare Tuberous Thistle was discovered within the grounds. A perennial of lowland calcareous soils, in Wales it now survives in only a handful of sites along the Glamorgan coast. The grass is left uncut during the spring and summer to allow it to grow and seed.

More information: For more details, see www.nashpoint.co.uk, or phone 07850 047721

> *"The lighthouse has shone its light every night since September 1st, 1832"*
>
> Trinity House

Seaside home: *A whitewashed cottage hugs the back of Tresilian Bay*

Inside are copies of 16th-century painted panels depicting the Stradlings, who held St Donat's for more than 400 years, and an interesting lectern with a revolving book holder supported on a figure of St John the Evangelist.

St Donat's Castle was built by the de Haweys, who also owned lands across the channel in Somerset. The castle passed to the Stradling family through marriage and remained occupied until the 18th century. Some renovation was undertaken during the 19th century before William Randolph Hearst, the American newspaper magnate took up residence in 1925. Money was no object in his restoration of the estate and for a few years he entertained the rich and famous. However, Hearst's fortunes waned and before he could sell the castle, it was requisitioned for the war effort. In 1962 it was bought for the Atlantic College, which attracts students from around the world and was the first United World College.

At the concrete quay, keep ahead, dipping across a slipway. Towards the far end of the quay, follow a path climbing into the trees. After briefly emerging at the edge of fields the way continues through more clifftop woodland. Ignore a crossing path, but a little further on, a steep path is signed down to the rocky beach for those wishing to investigate. Otherwise, keep ahead to leave the wood through a kissing gate.

The **official route** of Wales Coast Path, however, lies to the right, quickly swinging left to continue above the cliffs. The views are initially obscured by a wall of thorn thicket crowning the edge, but reaching a remnant of stone wall, there is a fine prospect back to St Donat's.

After passing a Second World War bunker, steps lead down to Tresilian Bay, where the pebbles have been swept into terraced shelves above the wave-washed bedrock. Walk across the head of the stony beach and climb steps past another bunker to regain the cliffs. There are more fine views, but all too soon, the path drops again into Cwm Col-huw, where there is a car park, toilets and a beach café at 6.

Detour: *To Llantwit Major*
A path along the north side of the valley or the lane from the car park lead into **Llantwit Major** 1½ miles/2.5 kilometres away, where there are two pubs, accommodation, shops and other services.

Sea-rounded boulders sit on a wave-cut limestone platform

Section Five

Llantwit Major to Barry Island

Distance: *12 miles/19.5 kilometres* | **Start:** *Col-huw Point car park SS 956*
Finish: *Junction of A4055 with The Parade ST 106 668* | **Maps:** *Ordnance Survey Landranger 170 Vale of Glamorgan and 171 Cardiff & Newport OR Explorer 151 Cardiff & Bridgend*

Outline: Another day of undulating clifftop paths, with occasional steep gradients but otherwise easy walking.

The path continues along the Glamorgan Heritage Coast, cutting in off the pebble beach along field edges to Limpert Bay. A walkway follows the sea wall around Aberthaw Power Station to a small nature reserve and the relics of a 19th-century limestone industry. Beyond Rhoose Point, the most southerly point of mainland Wales, the way runs along the edge of Porthkerry Country Park. A run of cliffs leads to the beach by Cold Knap Point before taking to the streets, skirting Barry Harbour and following the causeway road onto Barry Island.

Services: *Llantwit Major lies 1½ miles inland from Col-huw, but has accommodation and a range of shops and services as well as rail and bus services. There is accommodation at West Aberthaw and Gileston, with a café and toilets at Porthkerry Country Park. The popular resort of Barry Island has a range of shops, cafés and services and is served by both bus and rail. There is also a train station at Rhoose, with a linking path to the coast. Barry Island TIC 01446 747 171 | barrytic@valeofglamorgan.gov.uk*

👁 **Don't miss:** East Aberthaw Limeworks – lime kilns | **Rhoose Point** – southerly tip of mainland Wales | **Porthkerry Country Park** – 90 hectare woodland park

▲ *Col-huw beach*

Col-huw and Llantwit Major

Col-huw served as a landing for a religious college just inland at Llantwit Major. Originally founded at the end of the 4th century in the name of the Roman emperor Theodosius, it was re-established in the early 6th century by St Illtud. Its reputation as a centre of Celtic Christianity and Classical learning quickly spread and it reputedly could accommodate up to 2,000 scholars. St Samson, St Teilo, St David and St Patrick all spent time there and the community flourished for almost five centuries before falling prey to Vikings and then the Normans.

Given to Tewkesbury Abbey, it continued as a monastic outpost with a simple church built over the site of Illtud's Celtic chapel. The monks left at the Dissolution and the parish took over the eastern chapel and, although little remains of the monastic grange, the gatehouse and dovecote still stand. Inside the church is a collection of early carved stones and tomb slabs as well as some tantalising 15th-century wall paintings.

Although Llantwit expanded during the Second World War to support an RAF base at nearby St Athan, the old centre remains attractive and a town trail follows the winding, cobbled streets threading between its ancient buildings.

The Old Swan Inn sits at the heart of pretty Llantwit Major

The route: **Llantwit Major and Col-huw to Barry Island**

If you stayed overnight in Llantwit Major, return to the coast at **Col-huw**.

1 From the car park, a flight of steps zig-zag up and over **Castle Ditches** and a nearby Nature Reserve.

In the days when travel was often easier by sea than over land, the shingle beach at the foot of the Col-huw valley served as a landing for the scholastic settlement and abbey grange at Llantwit. From the 13th century, it would have been a useful asset to the Stradlings of St Donat's, who also held estates across the channel in Somerset. Old documents mention grain and other produce being exported around the coast.

Back on the cliffs, the path undulates at the edge of fields from which there are views across the perceptibly narrowing Bristol Channel, while revealed at low tide at the foot of the cliffs are curved and vividly striated bands of bedrock.

The uncultivated field margins are home to many wild plants and, in spring are streaked bright yellow with the flowers of gorse and wild cabbage. The tiny promontory of Stout Point gives a fine vantage along the cliffs towards the distant tall chimney rising above the Aberthaw Power Station.

The path eventually leads to a building that was used recently as a coast-guard lookout and a Seawatch Centre, but is now closed.

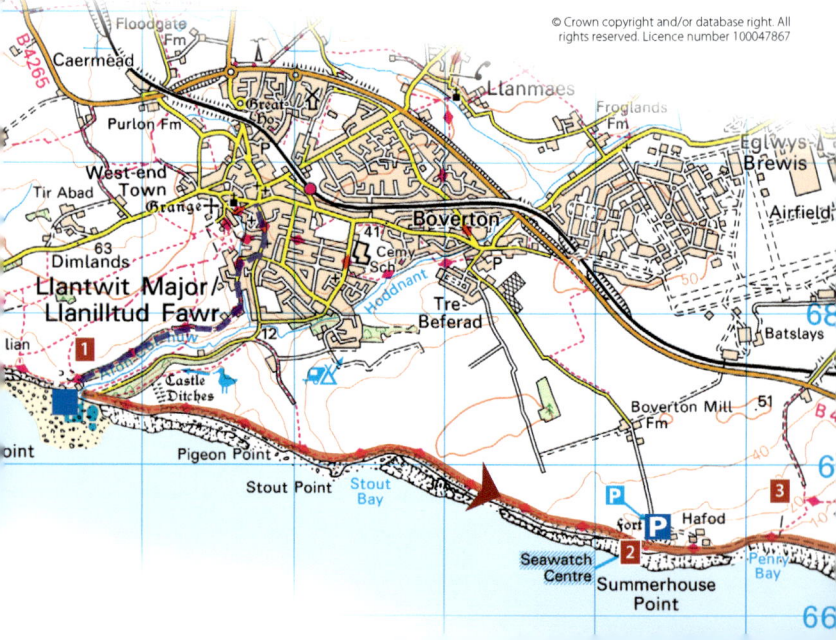

© Crown copyright and/or database right. All rights reserved. Licence number 100047867

Section 5: **Llantwit Major to Barry Island** 127

Oh, I do like to be: *Limestone cliffs and boulders at Col-huw beach*

2 Beyond the building, the path delves into a thicket tunnel, heaving abruptly over the emphatic triple embankments of an **Iron Age fort**, which is otherwise hidden by scrub.

Summerhouse Point *takes its name from an 18th-century octagonal summerhouse built within the Iron Age fort to exploit the views across the Bristol Channel and whose overgrown ruin is hidden in the trees. The adjoining cottage housed the caretaker and was lived in until the 1920s.*

(The path to the left leads to a small car park and further on, the small village of Boverton with shops and other services.) Back at the coast path, carry on, dropping steeply to emerge on a **cobble beach**, which is defended by a nearby cylindrical **Second World War bunker.** Walk on at the beachhead for 200 metres to find a waymark directing the path through scrub to the field behind. Continue at its edge to a kissing gate in the corner.

3 The onward path keeps to the coast, behind the pebble embankment. Carry on along several field edges, through gates and bridges to **Limpert Bay**. *Emerging into view are a long line of concrete blocks, Second World War defences (called 'the Walls') placed to hinder enemy tank landings.* Carry on along an uncultivated strip where brackish pools and wildflowers attract birds, butterflies and other inscts. Approaching the power station, bear right through a gate between the anti-tank blocks and wind past a **ruined building** to a **car park** at 4. Head across the **coastal car park** beside **Aberthaw Power Station** and turn right onto the concrete perimeter path.

Detour: *To Gileston village*

Well worth a visit, the pretty village of Gileston is a short walk up the lane from the car park.

The Giles family held the manor in the 14th century, giving their name to the small settlement of Gileston. The original church by the manor house was named for St Mabon, a brother of St Teilo, but when the church was rebuilt around 1450, it was rededicated to St Giles, the patron saint of cripples. The church is renowned for its well-preserved oak door, still swinging on original hinges and incorporating the heraldic shields of local families: Walsh, Umfraville, Fleming, Cradock and of course Giles.

The lords of the manor and later, the government, derived considerable income from all the local trade in the form of customs dues and an officer was posted to oversee the port and collect the fees.

Inevitably there were those intent on circumventing the system and, during the 17th century, smuggling was big business, particularly in tobacco from the West Indies. Meeting small local vessels out at sea, landing cargo on deserted beaches or bribing port officials to turn a blind eye to the true amount unloaded was

Wind-trimmed scrub rims the shallow cliffs above Penry Bay

Sea clatter: *The broad, pebbly beach at Limpert Bay*

common. Like today, the smuggling business was encouraged by the imposition of high taxes, but penalties for getting caught were severe; boats and equipment could be seized and smugglers and their accomplices could face heavy fines, deportation or even the hangman's rope.

4 The ongoing route follows a sea wall walkway around the perimeter of the power station. Although initially too high for short-legged walkers to peer over, the path soon rises and there are occasional ladder-ways giving views of the coast and access to the rocky foreshore. Around **Breaksea Point** the path winds to a partly enclosed area and bridge spanning the canalised outflow of the **River Thaw**.

Now escaping to the sea along a concrete conduit, the River Thaw looks the most unlikely of settings for a thriving port. Yet in the 17th century, it rivalled Cardiff for the number of ships coming and going. The shallow waters allowed only boats of up to 30 tons, but nevertheless there was a busy trade across the Bristol Channel to the markets of Minehead and Bristol. Lime and stone, cattle, farm produce, fish and oysters were staple cargoes and there was a healthy passenger trade too. And with agriculture one of the main occupations on both sides of the water, there was seasonal movement of labour, the south-facing Vale of Glamorgan's harvest coming ready just before that in north Somerset and Devon.

Several wealthy merchants based in Aberthaw commissioned their own ships, which were built from local timber. Their interests were not confined to the Bristol Channel and there was a healthy trade with Ireland, France, Spain and even the West Indies, dealing in sugar and tobacco. Fully laden larger ships like the 100-ton Great Thomas were too big to be handled here, but would first unload a part cargo at Minehead before crossing to Aberthaw. This in turn provided business for small tenders to ferry goods back and forth and such constant trade meant that English was commonly spoken in the area

The first power station at Aberthaw was built in 1966 beside the mouth of the River Thaw on the Leys: dunes and burrows that were once used as a golf course. When built, it was the most advanced station of its type and continued in service until 1995. The plant was then decommissioned, its two towering chimneys finally demolished in 1998. Aberthaw B (now closed) was already up and running, having come on line during the early 1970s. Replacement with a nuclear power station had been considered, but instead, the coal and biomass fuelled plant has been environmentally upgraded to reduce emissions and is running a trial for carbon capture. The curious domed concrete structure out to sea is a 'caisson', or intake, to collect cooling water for the condensers.

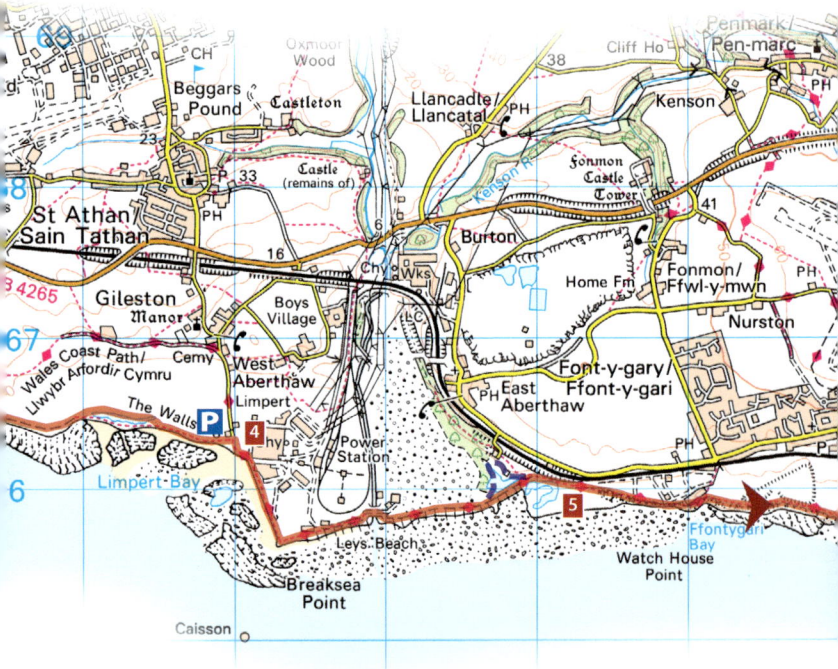

Beyond the bridge, the path runs below once-stark mountains of pulverised fuel ash, waste from the power stations. Now landscaped, they are slowly beginning to naturalise and scrub is already developing at the margins. The poor soil encourages masses of less common flowers, particularly orchids and helleborines.

Eventually the bordering fence ends and the land opens to the left, gently falling to a large, reed-filled pond.

Detour: *To the ruined East Aberthaw limeworks*

A short diversion on a path around the pool is well rewarded, both in the wildlife to be seen and the impressive ruin of the former 👁 **East Aberthaw limeworks** that rises almost fortress-like behind. It helps give context to the huge, abandoned quarries soon to be encountered a little further on along the coast.

The local lias limestone was noted as a source of hydraulic lime and considered by Joseph Smeaton as the basis for a concrete that would set underwater, when he was commissioned to build the third lighthouse on the Eddystone Rocks in 1756. In the end, however, he apparently settled for lime

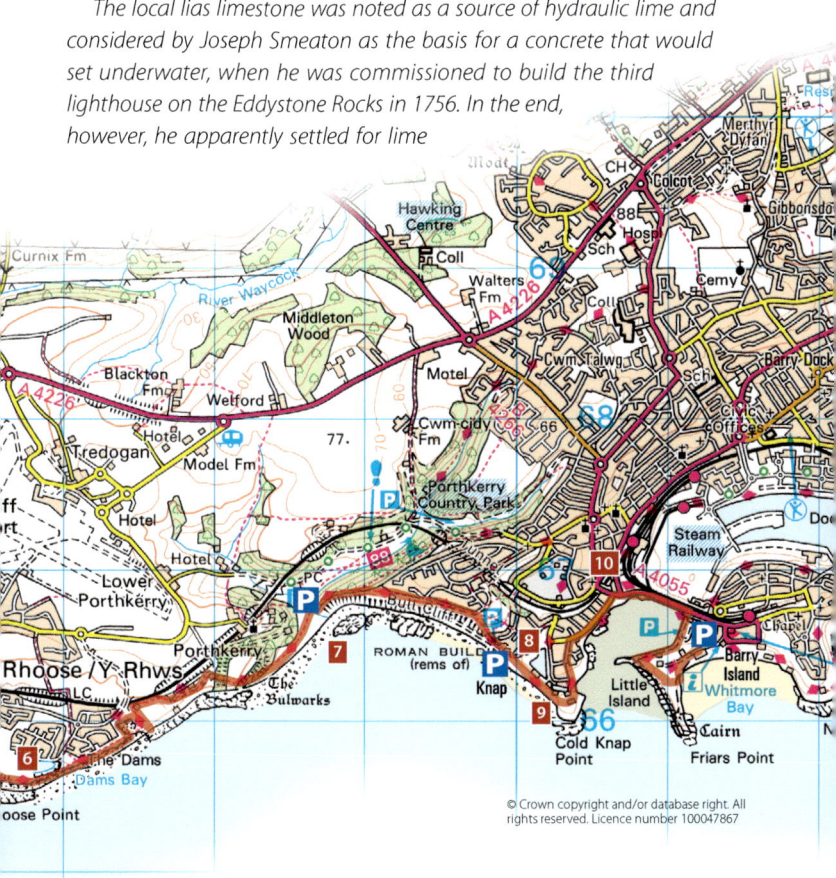

All that remains: *The massive walls of the once busy East Aberthaw limeworks*

from Watchet on the other side of the Bristol Channel. Nevertheless, by the end of the 19th century, Portland cement was big business and, with ready access to coal, the Aberthaw Pebble Limestone Company opened in 1888, the kilns initially burning beach pebbles. The plant operated until 1926 and remains in a remarkable state of preservation. Until recently, cement was still made at Aberthaw, just a short way inland, the stone coming from an adjacent quarry.

Back on the **official route**, the coast path runs behind a short concrete breakwater, past several groynes, and up steps to the beachhead, where **brackish pools and dunes** trapped behind the shingle provide another unexpected wildlife habitat. Continue ahead beside the lagoons for 200 metres, then take the steps on the left winding up the scrub-clad cliffs. *Their height opens a panorama across the channel to Somerset and Devon.* Reaching a junction at the top of the steps, turn sharp right, climbing more easily beside a **railway** to emerge through a gate at the edge of a **caravan park**.

5 Remain by the right-hand perimeter hedge, to pass a gated path that leads down to the beach. Continue past steps down to the rocky beach and a promontory viewpoint overlooking **Ffontygari Bay**. *A short walk up steps to the left are a caravan park, fish and chip shop, and the Fontygary Inn.* From the viewpoint, climb the steps ahead. Skirt the edge of a field, cross a bridge and head up steps to a perimeter fence. *The path on the left by the bridge heads up to the railway station and town of Rhoose, with shops and other services.*

Climb the steps ahead to continue along the cliff, shortly passing the first of a succession of **quarries** that have exploited the extensive limestone deposits in this part of South Wales.

The line of quarries along the coast below Rhoose illustrates the huge demand for hydraulic cement and concrete during the Victorian period. In particular it was used for many of the new docks being built around the country, including those at Liverpool. The smaller quarries were worked directly into the cliff face, but the larger sites were dug behind, the cliff wall offering some protection to the workings. After burning in kilns, the lime was loaded to ships waiting on the beach below.

Although the first quarry passed appears large, the second, behind Rhoose Point is truly vast and was worked until the early 1990s. More recently, the area has been reclaimed and, as well as accommodating a residential estate contains a large lagoon and several ponds, with the surrounding area being managed as a variety of wildlife habitats and a landscape sculpture park. Rhoose Point is

A loading gap quarried into the cliffs at Rhoose Point

the most southerly tip of mainland Wales (although at low tide you can wander out further from Breaksea Point) and a slate monolith has been erected beside the path to celebrate the spot.

6 Beyond 👁 **Rhoose Point** the way becomes enclosed in thicket, dropping steeply to the foot of a grassy fold behind the beach. Climbing beyond, the view opens to Bull Cliff and Barry Island before the path swings inland around the head of another quarry to emerge onto a service road by the **ruin of a large lime kiln**.

Follow the road left and right around yet another **quarry**, this one now developed as a caravan site. Bear right past the parking area and then swing left along the central drive. As that later curves left, turn off right through a belt of trees that conceals the embankment of a large **Iron Age fort** known as the **Bulwarks**.

Although little remains visible today, the enclosure was defended by triple banks and ditches, with excavations revealing the location of at least three buildings and a period of occupation from around 700 BC until after the Romans left Britain in the 4th century. Until the 17th century the Bulwarks extended onto a small headland, but the Great Storm of 1607 caused a massive collapse of the cliff, the debris being washed east to form the long pebble beach that now runs to Cold Knap Point. The offshore rock exposed at low tide is a remnant of the cliff known as Castle Rock and supposedly was once the site of a lighthouse.

Cross the spacious enclosure, home now only to the outer landing lights

A summer rainbow arcs above Porthkerry viaduct

Cold, cold sea: *Looking back down Cold Knap Beach towards the Bulwarks*

of nearby **Cardiff Airport**, which lies less than ½ mile to the north, to pass into more woodland at the far side.

Cardiff Airport began life as RAF Rhoose — a training base for Spitfire pilots in 1941 — but was abandoned after the war. However, its potential was seen as a commercial airport and in 1952 it re-opened as Rhoose Airport with Aer Lingus operating a service to Dublin. A growing holiday charter business supported its steady expansion and in the 1970s Concorde made several visits, albeit with a minimal load. Further upgrades in the 1980s enabled it to take Jumbo Jets and Cardiff became the only Welsh airport running scheduled international flights as well as a main maintenance base for British Airways.

7 Dropping to a shingle beachhead, the path runs at the edge of 👁 **Porthkerry Country Park**, with a short walk inland to a café, toilets and car park.

Porthkerry Park was laid out in the 1840s by the Romilly family, who ran the estate as a model farm, building cottages for their workers and a sawmill to process timber from the surrounding woodlands. The woods cloaking the steeper slopes by Golden Stairs, however, have never been managed and are considered to be truly ancient. Amongst the trees has been found the very rare true service tree, thought to have died out in this country in the 19th century. It is a long-lived tree and can survive for up to 400 years.

Ancient layers: Looking along Cold Knap Beach towards Cold Knap Point

The local authority bought the estate in 1929 and have since managed it as a country park. However, during the Second World War, it was temporarily pressed into military service as an assembly depot for American equipment and troops prior to embarkation from Barry Docks as part of the Normandy landings.

Over to the left, striding across the valley is a **viaduct** built to carry the Vale of Glamorgan Railway.

Dominating the western valley is an imposing 13-arch viaduct, built to carry a railway connecting the docks at Barry with the Bridgend coalfield. Work began in 1894, but was bedevilled by subsidence. Some said the whole thing should be dismantled and rebuilt from scratch, but in the end major repairs were undertaken and it was reopened in 1899. It remains in constant use today, carrying the main South Wales line.

Alternative route: *Along the beach*
If the tide is safely out, you can walk along the pebbly beach below Bull Cliff all the way to Cold Knap Point.

But to continue on the **official path**, when you reach an intersecting path, swing left over a bridged ditch then bear right over a second bridge. Go left and then branch right up a stepped path known as the **Golden Stairs**, supposedly referring to a pirate's treasure that has yet to be found. Climb along a narrow, wooded ridge that separates the sea from the cwm behind to a fork. Take the right branch, shortly emerging onto an open green above **Bull Cliff.** The way continues beside clifftop thicket, which, although helping reduce erosion, does nothing for the view. As the way eventually falls ever more steeply towards **The Knap,** Barry Island appears ahead. Finally,

Roman Villa?

Cold Knap Point is thought to have been a Roman port. The building by the path dates from around AD 300. Although described as a villa, its use is uncertain and the lack of a hypocaust — or central heating system — suggests it was a public rather than a private building. It was certainly built to impress, with limestone walls and ceramic roof tiles. Yet, oddly, archaeological evidence shows it was never completed.

Where we walked: *Looking back down Cold Knap beach*

steps and a concrete path drop beside seafront houses and flats, passing the excavated **foundations of a Roman villa** towards the bottom, which is discretely set back behind a viewing platform.

8 The Path emerges at a small roundabout by the entrance to a car park, where there are **toilets** and a **beach shower**. *If you turn left at the roundabout, you'll find a few cafes.* At the roundabout, continue along the promenade past the **Marine Lake**, dug in the shape of a Welsh harp. At the far end, a path winds around the small, grassy head of **Cold Knap Point**, merely bringing you back to the **promenade** where you started, but enriched by the view.

At one time, Cold Knap Point was a small island used as a burial ground in the Iron Age. During the medieval period, its limestone was quarried for the castle at Barry, but by the early 20th century, Cold Knap had become a popular beach resort, drawing crowds from the nearby mining villages. One of its attractions was Bindles Ballroom, which opened in 1928. It had a reputation as the best dance floor in South Wales and functions had to be booked two years in advance. The last dance was in 1982 and the site has since disappeared beneath a block of flats.

9 Continue past the **lifeguard station** and swing left above **Watch House Bay** to a vehicle barrier.

*The small tower overlooking the bay is known as the **Watchtower** and was built around 1865 to house a lifeboat. A second building on the cliff behind was used to store rescue rockets and other paraphernalia to assist craft driven onto the coast. After the construction of Barry Docks, the lifeboat was transferred there in 1901 and the Watchtower has since been used as a café and headquarters for Sea Scouts.*

Cross the turning circle to a stepped path opposite, which emerges onto the corner of a street. Keep ahead along **Cold Knap Way** and, at the top, go right along **The Parade** past a small park overlooking the **old Barry harbour** to a mini-roundabout overlooked by **The Ship** at `10`.

The Watchtower once housed the local lifeboat

SECTION SIX

Barry Island to Cardiff Barrage

Distance: *15 miles/24 kilometres (9 miles/14.5 kilometres using bus)* | **Start:** *Junction of A4055 with The Parade ST 106 668* | **Finish:** *Cardiff Barrage car park ST 190 724* | **Maps:** *Ordnance Survey Landranger 171 Cardiff & Newport OR OS Explorer 151 Cardiff & Bridgend*

Outline: Beyond Barry Island, docks and industry push the route inland, but after Sully Bay it is easy walking by the coast all the way to Penarth.

Barry Island has a couple of fine beaches, but the ensuing road walk skirting Barry's docks and coastal industry has little merit. Unless determined to walk every step of the way, it is best avoided by catching a bus to Sully. Beyond, the route largely sticks with the coast and is once more pleasant above low cliffs and rocky shores. After rounding Lavernock Point, it rises over higher ground to the resort of Penarth and the southern end of the Cardiff Bay Barrage.

Services: *Barry, Barry Island, Sully, Penarth and Cardiff all have a great variety of shops, cafés, accommodation and other services, also good bus and train links.*

👁 **Don't miss: Jackson's Bay** – Barry Island's secluded beach | **Sully Island** – tidal island once used by smugglers | **Lavernock Point** – site of Marconi's radio experiments | **Penarth Pier** - cinema, cafes, sweet shop and seasonal boat trips

▲ *Barry Island promenade*

Barry Island

Until the late 19th century, Barry Island was indeed an island, accessible by stepping stones at low tide. Bronze Age people used it as a burial ground and, during the early centuries of Celtic Christianity, its isolation attracted a monastic community under St Peiro, becoming a place of pilgrimage after St Baruc's body washed up on the shore. He had drowned while retrieving a sacred book from Flat Holm.

Although a base for Viking raiders and medieval conyger or rabbit warren, the island was then largely ignored until the mid-19th century, when a house and pier built on Friars Point entertained passengers landing from the paddle steamers that plied the Bristol Channel ports.

Things took off when the railway opened for the 1896, August bank holiday, bringing 30,000 people to the beaches and small funfair. The resort rapidly expanded, surviving two World Wars to become the main holiday attraction on the South Wales coast. Billy Butlin's holiday camp, established in 1966, injected new life for another 30 years, before finally succumbing to competition from package holidays guaranteeing sun.

Today, the beach and funfair remain popular on sunny weekends and the 2007 BBC television series 'Gavin and Stacey' brought a sudden influx of new visitors.

Barry Island's traditional seaside attractions are a family favourite

The route: Barry Island and Barry to the Cardiff Barrage

1 Determined to miss nothing, the coast path follows the **causeway** onto **Barry Island**. Approaching the 'Welcome to Barry Island' sign, take a path off right that slopes down to the **harbour wall**. Walk away beside a car park. Reaching a **stone breakwater**, keep left towards **Friars Point**. The path soon swings again across the neck of the promontory, but you might wander out around the narrowing grassy headland for the views.

A natural haymeadow, Friars Point blooms yellow in spring with the dense flowers of cowslip and encourages crickets, grasshoppers, bees and hoverflies, including some rare species. During the 19th century it was used as a rabbit warren producing 18,000 pelts a year, which were shipped to Bristol where the fur was used in the manufacture of hats. The process of felt making involved the use of mercury which, over time, could be absorbed by the body and cause dementia, hence the term 'mad as a hatter'.

Either way, the paths combine on the eastern side of the headland to lead off Friars Point.

Leaving the headland behind, the path splits. The **official route** takes the higher path into the town, while the other drops onto a lower **promenade** around the head of **Whitmore Bay**.

Oh, I do like to be: *Whitmore Bay on Barry Island*

Detour: *Shoreline path around Nell's Point*
At low tide you can continue with the lower path at the back of **Whitmore Bay** and on along **Clements Colley Walk** around **Nell's Point** into the secluded cove of **Jackson's Bay**. At the far end of the beach, a steep path climbs out to **Redbrink Crescent** to rejoin the official route at Waypoint (**2**). However, the incoming tide floods the head of Jackson's Bay and the through route is only passable at low water.

On the **official route**, the higher path emerges onto the end of a street by the lodge gates to **Friars Point House**. Walk towards the resort, passing children's fairground rides before branching off in front of the **Smugglers Cove golf course** to follow the main path through the **promenade gardens**. Over a **footbridge**, the way rises onto **Nell's Point**. Keep right to reach the tip of the headland, there swinging sharp left with the higher path. After passing above a **National Coastwatch Centre**, carry on below houses overlooking 👁 **Jackson's Bay**. Towards the far end of the houses, an open park emerges. *If you want to visit Jackson's Bay, keep right.*

Jackson's Bay is named after Sir John Jackson who constructed the breakwater protecting the harbour entrance. It was originally called Breakwater Bay and it was only after the works had been completed that sand began to accumulate to create the sheltered sandy beach.

2 Head diagonally across the park to briefly join **Friars Road**. *At this point, it is worth a short detour left to visit the remains of St Baruc's chapel, after whom Barry is named.* Back at Friars Road junction, cross over to go straight on, then then turn left and cross over **Breaksea Drive** to head back to the resort. Past the **train station** and a restaurant, bend around past **Maslin Park**. Cross Plymouth Road at the traffic lights, then head to **Clive Road** to join **Ffordd y Mileniwm**. Keeping to the right side of the road, cross several side roads and continue past the superstore to cross **Neptune Road**.

Alternative route: *Catch the bus to Sully*
To avoid a long road walk to Sully Bay, you can catch a bus from Barry Island (No. 95) into town, changing by the Morrisons store on Millennium Way onto bus No. 94 and alighting at **Sully Church** on **South Road** (near **4**). Then, either walk back to pick up the **official route** at the **roundabout** or walk a little further along to find a **short-cut footpath** leaving on the right beside houses to the coast.

After 200 metres, bear right along a pleasant **quayside promenade**

Enjoying the funfair at Barry Island

Seaside holiday: *Looking back across Whitmore Bay from Nell's Point*

overlooking the western basin of **Barry Docks**. Approaching the far end, leave left up the last street, **Cei Dafydd** and keep ahead to rejoin **Ffordd Y Mileniwm**. Cross to the opposite footway and turn right past the imposing 19th-century **Dock Offices**, now used by the Vale of Glamorgan Council. Behind this is a train station and car park. *The* **statue** *in front is of David Davies who spearheaded the 19th-century dock development.*

3 Over a **roundabout**, keep ahead along **Ffordd y Mileniwm** (shared use) for ¾ mile/1 kilometre to another **roundabout**. Again continue forward, now passing houses and light commercial units. Keep right with the main road as it shortly splits, following it for another ½ mile/800 metres. At traffic lights past **Dow Corning**, the road becomes a dual carriageway, with oncoming traffic. Just before the next roundabout, bear right along a short lane that emerges onto the **B4267** towards Sully. Take care crossing the busy road.

Although close to Barry, there was also a castle at Sully, founded around 1039 by the Norman, Reginald de Sully. He was one of the legendary Twelve Knights of Glamorgan who took the region from the Welsh under Robert Fitzhamon, and the family held the manor until the line died out in the middle of the 14th century. The castle was then abandoned and only a fragment of wall survives beside the church, with which it is contemporary.

Barry Docks

Barry Docks

Brainchild of the industrialist David Davies

Barry claims a long history; Romans and Vikings used it as a base, there were early Christian connections and the Normans established a small castle. Yet it was not until the 17th century that it achieved prominence as a port, trading around the channel and into France. Smuggling and piracy injected occasional colour, but by the 19th century, the old harbour was busy exporting limestone, coal and local produce, which included rabbit pelts to the hatters of Bristol.

But, as with other ports along this coast, it was the Industrial Revolution's insatiable demand for Welsh coal that prompted the greatest change. As early as 1865 it had been proposed as an alternative to Cardiff's then expensive facilities. However, it was not until 1884 under the leadership of the wealthy industrialist and politician David Davies that work began on transforming the tidal sound between the mainland and island into a fully serviced dock. By 1914, the port had outstripped Cardiff, handling over 11 million tons of coal a year. It had a strategic role during two World Wars, playing a key role in landing American equipment before the D-Day landings.

Although hard hit by the subsequent decline of the coal industry, it remains a vibrant port. Redevelopment is creating new leisure, residential and commercial areas, while the eastern docks continue to serve local industries.

Green and grey: *The coast path follows the pebbly shore towards Sully Island*

4 Just before the next roundabout, cross at the island crossing to turn right along **Hayes Road**. *Just behind Sully Church is the Sully Inn*. After ½ mile/800 metres, just after a lay-by where a snack van is sometimes parked, look for a stile on the left from which a path cuts between paddocks to emerge at the coast at **Sully Bay**.

Detour: *To see some of Wales' best dinosaur footprints*

At **5***, wander some ¾ mile/1.2 kilometres along the coast to the west and you'll come to* **Bendrick Rock***, where some of the best dinosaur footprints in Wales are exposed at low water. Some 220 million years old, they date from the dawn of the dinosaur age and are of several species including a small, upright, three-toed carnivore and a larger four-toed plant-eating animal that walked on all fours. Good examples can be seen in Cardiff's National Museum.*

Despite its proximity to industrial and urban life, the coast supports a surprising variety of wildlife. Migrant and overwintering birds such as oystercatcher, curlew, ringed plover and turnstone probe the shoreline mud and weed for food, whilst surviving amongst the dry shingle, plants such as sea radish, samphire and sea beet are to be found.

5 However, the **official route** of the coast path runs away to the left, initially fringed by a high wire fence. Carry on across a **slipway** and later behind the houses and recreation facilities of **Sully** above a **rocky apron** exposed at low tide. Eventually, after 1¼ miles/2 kilometres and heading a little inland around a caravan site, a waymark directs you out through a kissing gate onto a lane. Turn right past a caravan park back to the coast at **Swanbridge Bay**, where you will find the **Seashore Grill, On the Rocks Bar**, a car park, and a pub - **The Captain's Wife**.

The captain in question lived in one of the cottages integrated within the present pub. Despite the taboo of having a woman aboard ship, his wife accompanied him on one of his trips. Sadly she died during the voyage and, to avoid upsetting his superstitious crew further, the captain concealed her body in a chest. On his return home, he hid the chest while arranging a proper funeral. However, when he came to retrieve it, the chest had gone, presumably stolen by one of the crew thinking it might be treasure. Her ghostly spectre is one of several said to wander around the pub.

Detour: *Low-tide visit to Sully Island*
Low tide reveals a rocky causeway to 👁 **Sully Island**, but <u>take great care if you cross</u>; passage is only safe for a couple of hours either side

The popular Captain's Wife pub is close to the coast

Islands in the stream: *The coast looks out to Flatholm and Steepholm in the Bristol Channel*

of low water after which it is quickly flooded by a strong and treacherous current. Check the RNLI tide times safety warning system on the boundary wall by the On the Rocks Bar.

Archaeology has revealed a Bronze Age burial and a Saxon enclosure on the island as well as traces of visits by Romans and Vikings. Indeed three separate hoards of Roman coins were discovered nearby in 1899 and 2008. The island's lee created a sheltered landing, which served a small fishing fleet as well as traders landing goods in later centuries. Being out of the way, some tried to avoid paying customs dues and it was said that there was a smugglers' tunnel from Sully House to the island.

6 Through a gap at the far side of the **car park**, continue on the **official route** along a **seafront lane**. After climbing above **wooded cliffs**, it winds from the shore. A coastal footpath shown on maps has fallen with the cliff into the sea, so you must continue for another ¼ mile/400 metres past **Bay Caravan Park**.

7 Just beyond the top entrance to the site, leave through a kissing gate on the right and follow the boundary back through a couple of fields behind the park. Over a **footbridge**, swing right and then left through trees to the cliffs. The ongoing path is left, but it is worth first going right for a view across the bay. The path winds on past the **remains of a gun battery** before turning in again behind another caravan site.

*Known as **Lavernock Fort**, the gun emplacement was originally established in 1870 to protect the approaches to the ports and shipyards at Bristol and Cardiff. The 'fort' was upgraded during the First World War with former naval guns and augmented by a searchlight battery during the Second World War. Together with batteries on the Somerset coast and the islands of Flat Holm and Steep Holm, it gave protection to the Severn Estuary ports against sea and air attack.*

Pier group: *The view along the coast from Lavernock Point towards Penarth Pier*

Passing through a gate, bear right and follow the edge of a small **nature reserve** to emerge onto a lane. Go right, passing a small church. Continue along a gravel path to regain the coast at 👁 **Lavernock Point**.

The few unimproved fields behind the caravan site are protected as a small grassland nature reserve. Amongst the wildflowers to be found are knapweed and fleabane, which attract bees and other insects including many species of butterflies. In fact 20 of the 60 species known to breed in Britain have been found here.

The small church at the end of the lane is open occasionally and run by the St Lawrence at Lavernock Trust for special services, including 'Sea Sunday'. Look on the churchyard wall to find a plaque commemorating Marconi's first transmission of radio signals across open sea. After two days of abortive efforts, he achieved two-way Morse communication with a radio on Flat Holm island in May 1897. A week later, the experiment was repeated between Lavernock and Brean Down on the other side of the Bristol Channel. Within three years, radio was being installed on ships, but largely for the convenience of passengers. It was not until the Titanic disaster in 1912 that its importance to maritime safety was appreciated and the discipline of formal radio watches and reserved distress frequencies were adopted.

8 The path continues north, passing a small **Gothic tower** overlooking the beach. Beyond, the views are largely obscured by thick scrub, but approach-

Victorian delight: *A gull's-eye view of Penarth Pier*

ing **Cosmeston**, watch out for the entrance to a Cold War **underground bunker** hidden beside the path.

With the onset of the Cold War, Civil Defence entered a new era with the construction of underground bunkers to serve as shelters, nuclear detectors and command centres. One was constructed on the coast here and brought into manned operation for 10 days during the Cuban Missile Crisis of 1962.

Soon after, the path emerges onto a **clifftop green**. Follow it on for ¾ mile/1.2 kilometres before joining the seafront road through **Penarth**.

Penarth is unlike the other coastal towns so far passed on the South Wales section of the Coast Path. Although developing during the 19th century both as a seaside resort and dock town, it managed to separate its two characters and retain an air of exclusiveness. This was partly due to its ownership by the Earls of Plymouth who greatly influenced the town's layout, creating impressive public buildings and incorporating parks and open spaces. So much so, it became known as the 'Garden by the Sea'. Its outlook across the Severn Estuary and separation from the industrial pall overhanging Cardiff and the valleys made it an ideal place to live for the area's wealthy businessmen, who built fine villas on the cliffs.

Inevitably, the sweeping beach attracted holidaymakers and several grand hotels opened to cater for their needs. The arrival of the railway in 1878 greatly expanded the trade, but also encouraged hoards of day-trippers from the mining towns in the valleys. Penarth's gentry were not impressed with 'the rabble from the hills' who were liable to go immodestly bathing in the sea without a costume.

👁 Penarth Pier *was completed in 1895, and served a ferry round to Cardiff as well as providing a stop for the pleasure steamers that plied across the channel. In 1907, a small wooden theatre was opened on the end, followed in 1930 by an Art Deco pavilion. But tragedy struck the following year when, on Bank Holiday Monday, a fire destroyed the theatre and part of the pier. The pier was repaired and carried on without the theatre until the SS Port Royal Park collided with it in 1947. Yet another accident occurred in 1981, this time it was the SS Bristol Queen that hit. However, repairs re-opened the pier on both occasions and a complete restoration began in 1994 with the fine pavilion restored to its former glory in 2013. Although lacking the gaudy entertainments of Barry Island, Penarth remains a popular destination, particularly with holidaymakers from the English midlands. Today, Penarth is widely celebrated as 'The Garden by the Sea'.*

Penarth Pier was voted 'Pier of the Year' by the National Piers Society in 2014

Over the water: *Penarth Pier was restored in the 1990s and is open all year round*

9 After passing the pier, the road turns uphill. Leave just past the bend up a stepped path on the right. Climb on along **Kymin Terrace** and then swing right into **Bradford Place**. At the top of the hill, go right again into **Clive Crescent**, passing through a gate at the end into a small park.

At the top, pause for a few moments at the viewing platform with its Wales Coast Path 'dragonshell' mosaic sculpture. Enjoy the view, too, which stretches on along the coast to the distant towers of the Severn bridges, some 25 miles/40 kilometres distant. It is also worth a short walk to Penarth town centre with its shops, cafes and other services; there are several ways to the town centre — look out for signs.

Leave through a gate on the left into a back street. At the end, turn right along **Clive Place** and keep with the main street as it winds left, right and then left again. After some ¼ mile/400 metres, just after a 'No Entry' street, double back sharp right down **Paget Road** to a small **roundabout** at the bottom.

The town's other half was centred on docks just around the point overlooking the estuary of the River Ely. Before the docks were constructed, the tidal river was already lined with wharves warehousing, coal yards and eventually railway sidings. There were even ship building and repair yards. But the demand for coal was so great that more facilities were needed, despite the proximity of Cardiff's docks. Work started in 1859 and the dock opened in 1865, a long curving pound paralleling the river, accessed from the sea through a locked basin. With ships queuing to enter, it was immediately successful. So efficient was the operation that rail wagons could deliver two loads a day from the collieries while ships could enter, be loaded and leave on the same tide. At its peak just before the First World War, it was exporting more than 4.5 million tons of coal a year.

Flatholm and Steep Holm

Standing at the mouth of the River Severn, the islands have been sporadically occupied since man's arrival in Britain. The Romans sited a signal station on Flat Holm and during the 6th century, they served as monastic retreats. But it was the Vikings who gave them their present names. Subsequently a landing for 18th-century smugglers and defences during the Napoleonic and two World Wars, they are now nature reserves.

Peering ahead?: *Looking east from Penarh Pier along the coast towards Cardiff Bay*

Like the other ports around the coast, Penarth was crippled by the post-war depression and despite the Earl of Portsmouth foregoing his dues, the docks closed in 1936. Yet three years later, it was open again to serve another war. In 1943, the US Navy 11th Amphibious Force moved in, using it as a base for the preparation of tank landing craft. The following year the docks were packed with invasion barges setting out for the Normandy beaches.

After the war, there was enough work exporting coal to keep the docks going for another 20 years before they were finally closed in 1963. A bund was built across the waist of the main dock, the western end being drained and used as a refuse landfill site. Following an expansive clean-up, the area has now been landscaped as a park. The seaward end and basin remained in water and were subsequently developed as a yachting marina, overlooked by an attractive housing development. Since the completion of the Cardiff Bay development project the marina accesses the sea via the massive freshwater lake and the three impressive Barrage locks.

After the third bridge to the right of the Barrier, stand on the yellow square to see the 'Three Ellipses' — a clever piece of public art by Swiss artist, Felice Varini.

Dereliction and demolition has lost some of Penarth Docks' landmarks such as the hydraulic powerhouse, which powered the cranes and lock gates and

Section 6: **Barry Island to Cardiff Barrage** 157

two subways, one of which tunnelled beneath the River Ely and the other passed beneath the dockland sidings before climbing a long flight of steps into the town. Remaining is the magnificent Customs House building, restored and used as a pub and restaurant. The French Renaissance style building next to it housed the dock offices and will hopefully be similarly rescued in the not too distant future.

Bear right to pass in front of the former **Customs House**, now a restaurant, and then wind left past a car park to the **locks and barrage** controlling maritime entry into **Cardiff Bay** at 10.

A yacht passing through the sea lock into Cardiff Bay

Section Seven

Cardiff Barrage to Newport

Distance: *20¾ miles/33.5 kilometres (18½ miles/30 kilometres if Transporter Bridge open) (13½ miles/22kilometres using bus)* | **Start:** *Cardiff Barrage car park ST 190 724* | **Finish:** *Newport Transporter Bridge ST 316 862* | **Maps:** *Ordnance Survey Landranger 171 Cardiff & Newport or OS Explorers 151 Cardiff & Bridgend and 152 Newport & Pontypool*

Outline: Cardiff Bay, a country park and the Wentlooge Levels more than compensate for the industrial part of Cardiff and urban entry into Newport. The long day begins with a walk around Cardiff Bay into the city, which presents the nation's capital at its best. However, you can be forgiven for catching a bus to avoid the trek through industrial suburbs back to the coast. The way then follows the Wentlooge Levels beside the narrowing Severn Estuary. Finally turning inland at the Ebbw River, the route is back on city streets into Newport. Some may opt for a bus, but smart planning will get you to the Transporter Bridge during opening hours to short-cut some of the town.

Services: *Accommodation, a full range of services and road and rail transport at both Cardiff and Newport. In between, there are pubs inland at St Brides and on the coast before West Usk Lighthouse, with accommodation at Ty-côch and St Brides. Cardiff TIC 029 2087 2167 | visitor@cardiff.gov.uk, Newport TIC 01633 842 962 | newport.tic@newport.gov.uk. See also:* **www.visitcardiff.com** *and* **www.cardiffharbour.com**

Don't miss: Cardiff Bay – the cultural, leisure and wildlife centre of the capital | **Tredegar House** – magnificent 17th century mansion | **Newport Transporter Bridge** – the oldest surviving such bridge in Britain (check for opening times)

▲ *Cardiff Bay*

Cardiff and its docks

Overlooking tidal estuaries and marsh, Cardiff's environs had been settled since the Stone Age. Both the Romans and Normans established strategic forts and by the 14th century, it was the largest town in Wales. But sacked by Owain Glyndŵr in 1404 and routed by the Parliamentarians during the Civil War, it awaited the Industrial Revolution to regain its supremacy.

Footing mineral-rich valleys, Cardiff was ideally placed to handle the insatiable demand for iron and coal. But its tidal wharves were overwhelmed until the first sea dock opened in 1839. The Taff Vale Railway followed a year later and the docks expanded to accommodate increasing trade. By 1907, Cardiff was the largest coal exporter in the world. The influx of labour settled in Butetown, which soon became known as Tiger Bay, a vibrant, multi-cultural community with a reputation for hard living.

Cardiff developed alongside its industry with fine public buildings, a university, parks and electric trams. Granted city status in 1905, it was declared the nation's capital in 1955.

But by then, coal was already declining, its fate set during pre-war strikes and depression. Coal exports ceased in 1964 and with the closure of Cardiff's steelworks in 1978, large parts of dockland were left derelict.

Cardiff Bay waterfront is a popular destination

The iconic Wales Millennium Centre on Cardiff Bay waterfront

Cardiff Bay

21st century gateway to a nation's capital

The opening of the Glamorgan Canal in 1794 gave the Merthyr ironmasters access to the sea through Cardiff. However, a lack of adequate berthing created a bottleneck, a problem exacerbated by the growing coal trade. The next century saw the port steadily grow with the opening of a succession of basins and docks around the bay. Within 50 years, the production of coal had overtaken iron and, by the beginning of the 20th century, Cardiff had become the world's largest coal port, exporting 9 million tonnes per year. Yet, despite its importance during two World Wars, by the end of the 1970s, much of the surrounding dockland had fallen into dereliction.

Renaissance began in 1987 with the formation of the Cardiff Bay Development Corporation, which was tasked with regenerating the old dockland. Originally, the bay had

Captain Scott memorial by Cardiff-based sculptor, Jonathan Williams

been a large tidal lagoon, exposing a vast expanse of saltmarsh and mudflats at low water. This meant that access to Cardiff's docks was limited to a couple of hours either side of high tide and had been one of the reasons for the rise of Penarth and Barry docks. The ambitious scheme put forward by the Development Corporation included a barrage to separate the bay from the open sea, creating a freshwater lagoon and eight-mile waterfront behind which rise smart, new building developments. However, the scheme was not welcomed by all; conservationists cited the loss of SSSI wetland habitats which were important feeding grounds for birds, while urban designer Adrian Jones, who grew up in the city, decried it as a 'dumb plan' and a contender for the 'worst example of waterside regeneration in Britain'.

But love it or loathe it, the scheme has completely transformed the bay. The half-mile barrage now impounds a 202-hectare freshwater lake fed by the Ely and Taff rivers. The head of the bay has been developed for leisure, retail, offices and housing, all of which is dominated by the National Assembly for Wales building and the Wales Millennium Centre. Three of the docks remain as working docks within the modern port, handling a variety of cargoes as well as having capacity to receive cruise ships, while the now land-locked West Bute Dock is the focus of a residential development. Locks give the several marinas within the bay access to the open sea and an 8-hectare wetland nature reserve is part compensation for the loss of the former extensive saltmarsh and mudflats. The first phase began with Atlantic Wharf, overlooking the West Bute Dock in 1990 and the barrage was finally completed in 1999.

The Senedd building, home of the Welsh National Assembly

> *"I wait in the evening air.*
> *Sea-birds drop down to the sea.*
> *I prepare to sail from where*
> *the docks' derelictions are"*
>
> Leaving Cardiff, *Dannie Abse*

More information: For more details, see: www.cardiffbay.co.uk

The route: Cardiff Barrage to the Wales Millennium Centre

1 Cross the barrage and follow a path on beside the service road, shortly passing a **white canopy** overlooking the waterfront.

It shelters a display commemorating the Scott Expedition's embarkation from Cardiff en route to the South Pole in 1910.

Scott named Cardiff as the home port for his ship Terra Nova in recognition of the funding and support the city gave to the expedition, much of it generated by 'Teddy' Edwards who claimed Welsh ancestry and was appointed Scott's second in command. Another Welshman whose heroic efforts contributed so much to the ill-fated venture was Edgar Evans. Born in Rhossili, Gower, he was a member of the polar party, but was the first to perish on the return, having suffered a serious head injury during a fall into a crevasse.

Having left London, Terra Nova made Cardiff its last call to take on coal and final supplies before heading south. Scott and his crew were overwhelmed with the city's welcoming generosity and were treated to a farewell dinner, officers at the Royal Hotel and the crew more modestly at the Barry Hotel as befitted the customs of the day. With promises to make Cardiff its first port of return, the Terra Nova left Roath Dock on 15 June 1910, spurred on by a cheering crowd. In the event, Scott and his four companions, disappointed with losing priority at the Pole to Roald Amundsen, perished, tantalisingly close to safety. Terra Nova did return to Cardiff almost exactly three years after its departure to be sold back to its original owners.

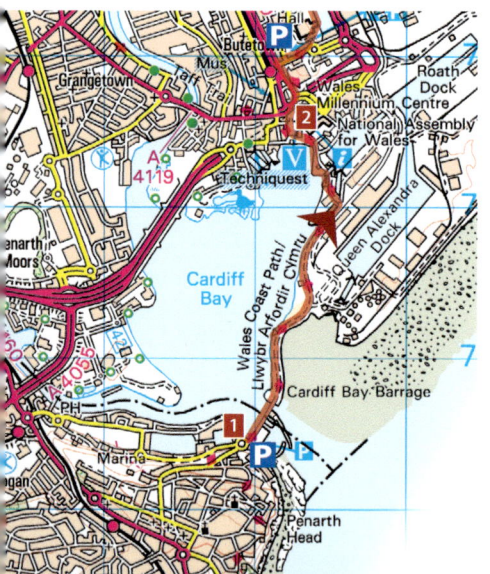

© Crown copyright and/or database right. All rights reserved. Licence number 100047867

To your left is the vast artificial lagoon of 👁 **Cardiff Bay**. Further along the **Barrage**, near the Roald Dahl 'Enormous Crocodile', an information board shows an augmented reality view of how the docks looked in their heyday. Just before the **Cardiff Sailing Centre** is a children's play area, skate park, and small **exhibit celebrating the South Wales coal mining industry**.

Barrage blues: *Huge counterweights dominate the barrage bridges*

Continue by the waterfront past a **graving dock** to a mini roundabout and swing left to pass a couple of cafés.

Carry on across a bridge spanning the lock entrance to the **Roath Basin** and past the **Norwegian Church Arts Centre**.

Walk on past the **Cardiff Waterside business complex** towards the imposing canopied entrance to **Y Senedd, the National Assembly for Wales**. Just beyond that is the 19th-century **Pierhead Building**, built as the headquarters for the Bute Dock Company.

Y Senedd, the National Assembly building was completed in 2006, its open design intended to symbolise participation in the democratic process. The complex incorporates committee rooms, offices and the Parliament's main debating chamber, overlooked by a public gallery. Beside is the Gothic Pierhead Building, constructed in 1897 between the entrances to the East and West Bute docks as the headquarters for the dock company, which was renamed that year as the Cardiff Railway Company. After the war, the building served the Port of Cardiff and is now a museum for Welsh history and a conference and debating centre. The clock tower bears an uncanny resemblance to the Clock Tower of Westminster Palace and is known as the Big Ben of Wales.

A waterfront sculpture celebrating the Welsh coal industry

Welsh coal

Fuel for the Empire

Extending over 100 square miles beneath the hills of South Wales is the largest coalfield in Britain. Although dug throughout history, it wasn't until the start of the Industrial Age in the 18th century that large-scale exploitation began. First mined to support the iron and steel industries that evolved in the valleys where coal and iron ore were found side by side, it later powered the Age of Steam.

Ports developed where the valleys converge on the coast, fed first by canals and then railways to take the coal to waiting ships. In a few decades, the Welsh coal industry grew to be the greatest in the world.

But nothing lasts forever. Cheap imports, economic depression, a general strike and falling demand all contributed to the industry's slow decline, taking with it the prosperity of the ports. By the second half of the 20th century, lack of investment and high costs left Welsh coal unable to compete. Pit after pit closed, culminating in a bitter confrontation between miners and Government. Today, although huge reserves remain in the ground, little is now mined, and most of what does see the light of day travels only as far as the Port Talbot steel works or the Aberthaw Power Station. In a world demanding green energy, there appears little future for coal, but the wheel may yet come full circle.

There turn right beside **Roald Dahl Plass**, passing a **statue of Ivor Novello** and the **Wales Millennium Centre**.

The sunken plaza behind the Pierhead Building commemorates popular children's author Roald Dahl, who was born in Cardiff to Norwegian parents in 1916 and christened in the White Church. The Plass occupies the site of the basin to the now infilled West Bute Dock, while nearby is a statue to the Cardiff-born popular composer and actor Ivor Novello. Overlooking all is the Wales Millennium Centre, an arts and theatre complex.

Looking across Cardiff Bay to the Grade I listed Pierhead building

Purple haze: *Nighttime reflections of the Wales Millennium Centre, on the Cardiff waterfront*

The route: **Millennium Centre to Newport Transporter Bridge**

Alternative: *Catch the bus to Pengam Green*

Initially, the next leg runs through an attractive city-centre development overlooking **East Bute Dock**, but beyond is the light industrial sprawl of **East Moors**. If you prefer to avoid a 5 mile-/8 kilometre-walk to the outskirts of the city, catch bus No. 8 from **Mermaid Quay** (outside the Cardiff Bay Visitor Centre) into the 'city centre' and change at **Wood Street** onto bus No. 11 to 'Pengam Green Tesco'. Alighting from the bus, walk out past the superstore car park to the main road, crossing on the lights to join the path at Waypoint (**5**).

2 Cross the main road on the traffic lights by the corner of the **Wales Millennium Centre** and walk forward behind the **Red Dragon leisure complex** along the broad boulevard of **Lloyd George Avenue**. Take the first right (**Cardiff Bay railway station** is over to the left) into **Hemmingway Road** and walk past a Travel Lodge. Approaching a roundabout, cross and go left towards **County Hall**. At another small roundabout in front of the building, swing right across a visitor car park before bearing left behind the building to continue along **Atlantic Wharf** beside the **East Bute Dock**.

West Dock, the first of Cardiff's docks ran parallel to the end of the Glamorganshire Canal. It closed in 1964 and was filled in five years later. The East Dock, close beside it remained operational until 1970 and the surrounding area eventually became the first to be developed as part of the Cardiff Bay regeneration plan. Once lined with warehouses and railway sidings, the western quay and the winding feeder canal became features in a housing development that became known as Cardiff's Little Venice.

Norwegian church

Cardiff was once a major port for the Norwegian merchant fleet and the White Church was built in 1869 as a Lutheran mission for its sailors. Originally clad in corrugated iron, it stood between the East and West Bute docks until it closed in 1974. It was dismantled and re-erected on the remodelled waterfront in 1992. Like the former mission church at Swansea, it is now used as an arts centre.

Immediately beyond a **Holiday Inn**, swing left and go over a **bridge** then left to walk on the canal-side. It winds on between waterside dwellings, eventually reaching a canal junction. Go right, cross the next **footbridge** and keep right to follow a street out to **Schooner Way** beside a Novotel. Head left to traffic lights.

3 Cross over by the traffic lights to turn right onto **Tyndall Street**. Crossing to the opposite footway, carry on past a roundabout beneath a flyover. Keeping left past the **'lightning' building**, carry on to the next roundabout and cross over at the pedestrian traffic lights, then re-cross **East Tyndall Street** onto **Ocean Way***, passing the Premier Inn and heading towards Newport. Follow the footway for ¾ mile/1.2 kilometres to a second roundabout and keep ahead, the path now only on the north side of the road. Continue over another large roundabout and a railway bridge just beyond to arrive at yet another roundabout. Go left, still towards Newport, but then cross to find a path leaving some 200 metres along on the right.

> *** Alternative:** *Tyndall Street to Rover Way*
> From the roundabout by Ocean Way, stay on East Tyndall Street past a superstore and onto Walker Road. Cross over Splott Road using the pedestrian crossing then turn left onto South Park Road and under a railway bridge. Passing the Health Centre, bear left into the park and walk

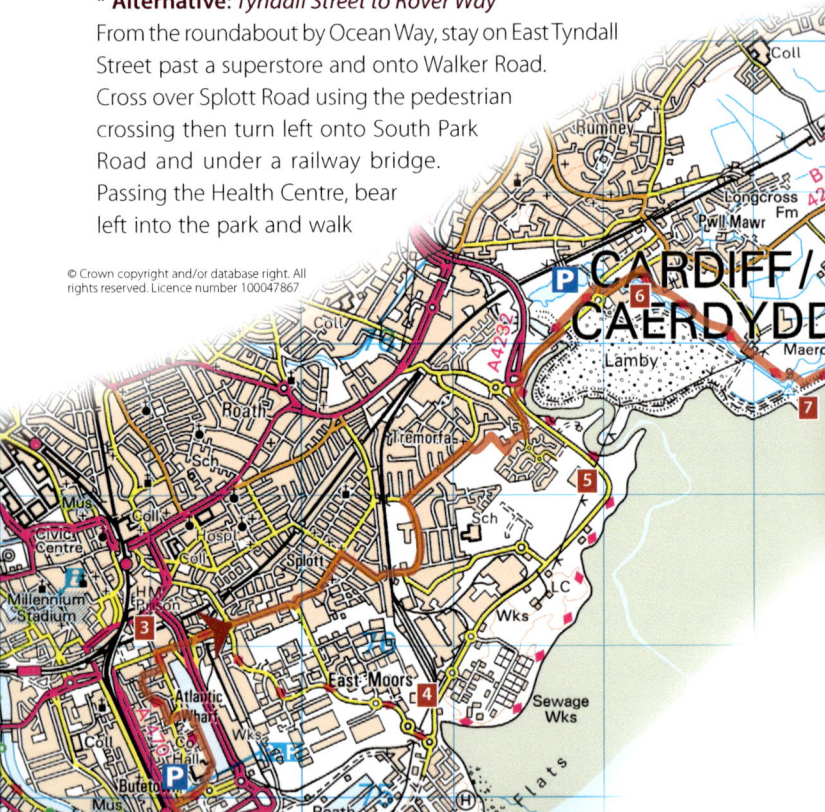

© Crown copyright and/or database right. All rights reserved. Licence number 100047867

Waterside homes: *Cardiff Dock's redeveloped western quay is now known as Little Venice*

along the path towards the Splott Community Hub building. At the Hub corner, leave the park and cross over Muirton Road on the pedestrian crossing and turn left. At the junction with Tweedsmuir Road, turn right and continue past shops. Look out for a lane on the right between the houses to head into another park. Once in the park, turn left and then right down the tree-lined path beside the playing fields. At the end of the path turn left and follow the footpath until you reach the road, Ffordd Pengam. Cross over the pedestrian islands to the opposite footway and continue straight on. Opposite a small business park, turn right onto the footpath and take great care to cross the island crossing over Rover Way. Turn left and follow directions to Parc Tredelerch (**5**).

4 A **cinder path** leads on around the coast, skirting industry before continuing around the scrub bank of a former landfill site that is slowly reverting to nature. Keep with the coast behind a small Travellers' site, the path then drifting to parallel the main road as it curves inland above the final meanderings of the **Rhymney River**. Some 300 metres beyond the bend, a faint path drops from the road by traffic lights at the entrance to a Tesco superstore. Those bypassing the city stretch by bus rejoin the path here.

Coastal flatlands: *The Usk Estuary viewed from high above the Wentlooge Levels*

5 Carry on, ignoring a track down to a boat store and shortly joining a **cycle track** that curves right to bypass a large roundabout. Cross the incoming road, **Lamby Way** and follow the path beside it across a bridge over the **Rhymney**. Immediately beyond the bridge, drop left into trees bordering **Parc Tredelerch**. Keep right as the path immediately forks, walking at the edge of rough meadows above a fishing lake. Emerging beside a car park, go right to a roundabout.

Prior to its reclamation and landscaping as a country park, this area beside the Rhymney River had been used for tipping waste. After two years of clearance, Parc Tredelerch was opened in 2003 and is centred upon a four-hectare lake that was originally a stranded oxbow bend of the river. It is now managed as a coarse fishery containing carp, perch tench and rudd. Birds to be seen on the water include coot, mute swan, great crested grebe and the ubiquitous mallard. There have even been sightings of a bittern amongst the reeds.

6 Turn left towards 'Wentlooge', crossing to the opposite footway. After 300 metres, just before an industrial unit, leave along a footpath on the right. Follow a **marshy reen** to the coast, winding over a couple of **footbridges** and through a boulder chicane up onto the **sea wall** that protects the **Wentlooge Levels** from flood.

7 Follow the **embankment path** for some 5¼ miles/8.5 kilometres before reaching the **Lighthouse Inn**. Shortly after this, the official route drops down to the track beside a reen to avoid disturbing overwintering birds, as part of the biodiversity restrictions on the Severn Estuary.

Please note: There are very few facilities on the Wentlooge Levels

Beyond the Tesco Store at Pengam Green facilities are few and far between. After 2¾ miles/4.5 kilometres, a waymarked path leaves across the fields to Peterstone Wentlooge, where there is an information board about the great flood of 1607. Some ¾ mile/1 kilometre further along the sea wall, a track turns off beside a large pool at **Peterstone Gout**, passing a golf club to reach the road, where a short distance to the right, Ty-côch Farm offers accommodation and camping. Another 1¾ miles/3 kilometres along the coast is the **Lighthouse Inn**, a popular pub on fine weekends. There is also an outdoor café and pay and display car parking. West Usk Lighthouse offers luxury bed and breakfast.

There is nothing beside the route through Newport, although you can catch a bus into the town centre near Duffryn High School or close to the underpass beneath the A48. Buses then leave the centre for Mariner Way on Felnex Industrial Park near the Transporter Bridge.

The diminutive West Usk lighthouse now provides luxury accommodation

Walk on for another mile/1.6 kilometres to **West Usk lighthouse**, where the route briefly returns to the embankment.

At only 55 feet tall and originally standing on an island until land reclamation pushed back the sea, West Usk must be one of the squattest lighthouses ever built. It was the first design by the Scottish engineer James Walker, who spent much of his working life on dock, harbour and canal projects and became Chief Engineer to Trinity House, producing another 21 lighthouses for them up and down the country. There is a tenuous link back to Cardiff's Pierhead Building in that Walker designed London's Big Ben tower. West Usk became operational in 1821 and guided shipping into the Usk for 100 years before being decommissioned in 1922. It subsequently served as a coastal lookout station during the Second World War and was more recently restored as a novel luxury bed and breakfast retreat.

8 Skirt the landward side of the **lighthouse** to a cattle grid. There, swing left as the official route again drops down to the track beside a reen. Ahead, the lattice towers of Newport's famous Transporter Bridge can be picked out amongst the pylons.

Across the river is the Uskmouth Power Station complex. Uskmouth 'A' ran on coal for 25 years from 1956 and was eventually demolished in 2002, making way for a gas-fired station that opened in 2010. The 'B' station came on line in 1961, but has had a chequered career and, despite being upgraded to one of the country's cleanest coal-fired stations, closed in 2014. There are currently plans to bring it back on-line under new ownership.

Reaching a soaring pylon, drop from the embankment (if you have not already done so) and follow the track inland beside the Usk's main tributary, the **Ebbw River.** Keep with the main track through a gate, shortly passing a junction from **New Dairy Farm** and ultimately crossing a **railway bridge** to the **B4239**.

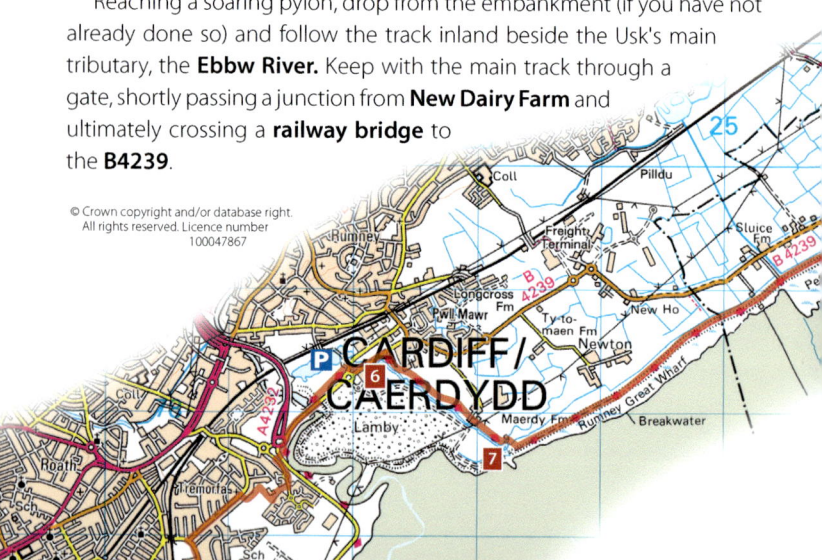

© Crown copyright and/or database right.
All rights reserved. Licence number 100047867

9 Go right and immediately right again over a **bridge** onto a contained path paralleling the road. Emerging opposite **Duffryn High School**, briefly follow the road on before leaving right, through a motorcycle barrier, along a footpath opposite **Heron Way**.

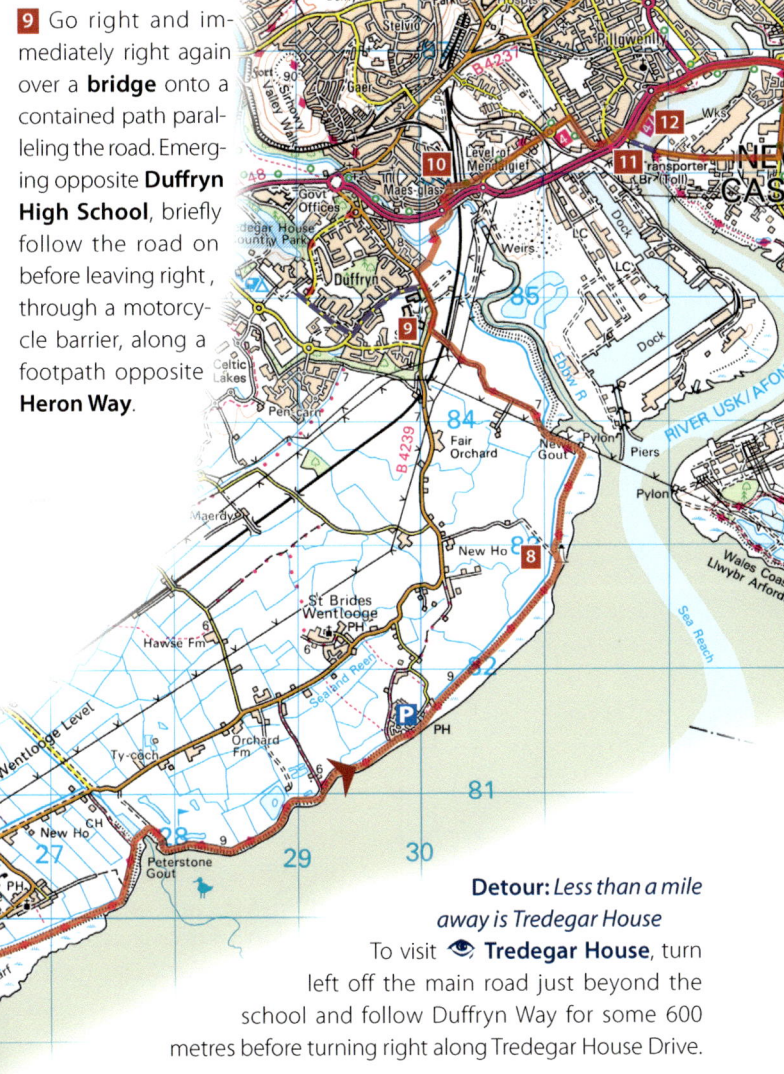

Detour: *Less than a mile away is Tredegar House*

To visit 👁 **Tredegar House**, turn left off the main road just beyond the school and follow Duffryn Way for some 600 metres before turning right along Tredegar House Drive.

Set within 36½ hectares of park and formal gardens, Tredegar House is one of the heritage gems of South Wales and is described as one of the most significant late 17th-century houses in Britain. The present house was built during the latter half of the 17th century for William Morgan, whose family had been dominant across South Wales since the 15th century and it

Grand facade: *Tredegar House and its park and gardens are now run by the National Trust*

was his successors who were the driving force in establishing Newport as a major trading port. The original house had been of stone, but the rebuilding was undertaken in red brick, a grand monument to emphasise the family's status. A later descendant, Godfrey Morgan was one of the fortunate few to return from the Charge of the Light Brigade. Subsequently the family's fortunes changed and in 1951 the house had to be sold, eventually being bought by Newport Council when it was dubbed 'the grandest council house in Britain'. Since 2011, it has been managed by the National Trust.

For the **official route**, continue beyond houses to a **bridge over the Ebbw** then skirt a rugby ground towards the main road (**A48**). Through an underpass, climb left and at the top, turn right to a path through a green, which later curves left. At the road, turn right over the railway bridge, then keep ahead where the road becomes a path, soon joining **Docks Way**.

10 Follow it past a retail park and beneath a railway bridge to a roundabout. Keep ahead to a T-junction and go right along **Mendalgief Road**. Bending left at the end, it comes out beside the **A48**. At a café, cross at the traffic lights towards the Waterloo Hotel, bear right to **Watch House Parade**, then head right at a break in the high fence. Cross on the pedestrian lights to the 👁 **Newport Transporter Bridge** at **11**.

Before 1906, Newport's only bridge spanning the River Usk was some 4½ miles upriver beside the castle, remote from the docks and poorly placed to support the industrial development of the eastern bank. A downstream alternative was needed, but a 47-foot tidal range and the need to allow unimpeded passage for shipping posed considerable difficulties. A ferry already operated at the chosen site, but the huge tidal range and swift current made it impractical for heavy use and a tunnel or swing and lifting bridges proved too costly.

*The solution lay in an 'aerial ferry', originally a British idea, but first realised when one was opened in 1893 across the mouth of the Nervion River in Bilbao. Following a visit to see another just completed in Rouen, the town council commissioned a transporter bridge for the Usk, one of only 21 ever built in the world. It operated for almost 80 years before wear and tear finally forced its closure in 1985. The crossing is an almost unique experience as there are now only six historical transporter bridges still operating world-wide, the only other one in Britain being across the River Tees at Middlesborough. To check opening times, see **www.newport.gov.uk/heritage** or call 01633 656656*

11 If the bridge is open you can cross the river straight to **12** and avoid 2 miles/3 kilometres of road walking.

Otherwise, there is no alternative but to follow the main road up to another roundabout. Turn right and continue beside the main road, crossing the **Usk** over **City Bridge** at **Spittles Point**. Reaching traffic lights at a large junction on the eastern bank, go right along **Corporation Road**. Pass beneath a railway bridge and then, after a further ¼ mile/400 metres, turn right again along **Stephenson Street**, which take you to the eastern portal of the **Transporter Bridge** at **12**.

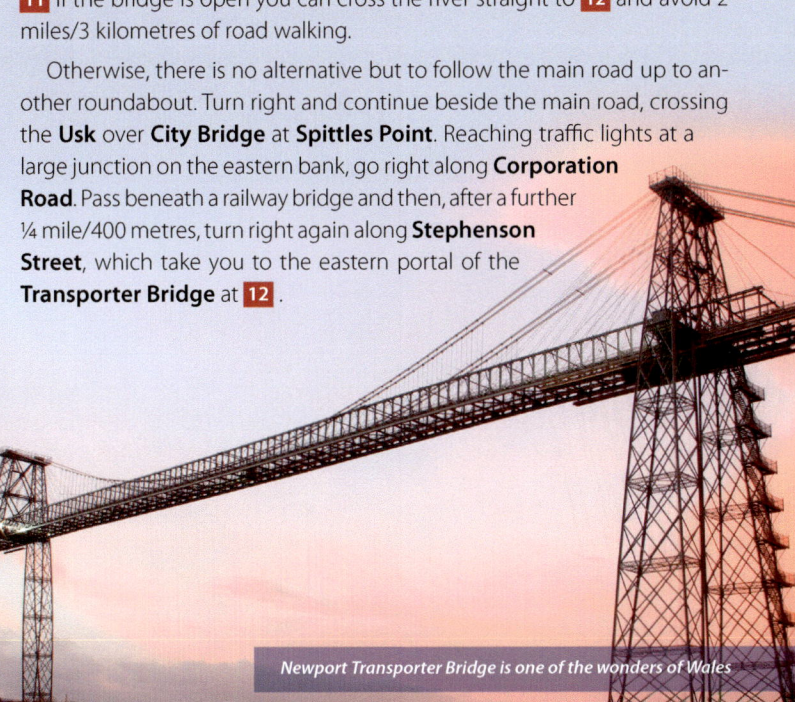

Newport Transporter Bridge is one of the wonders of Wales

Section eight

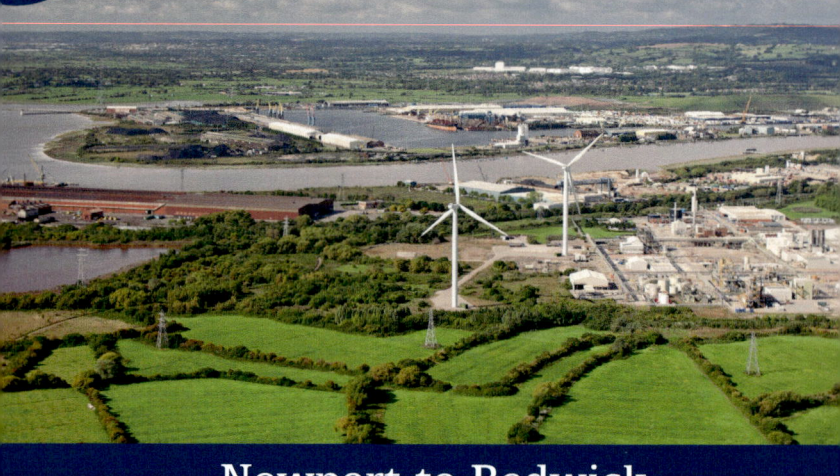

Newport to Redwick

Distance: *12 miles/19.5 kilometres* | **Start:** *Newport Transporter Bridge ST 316 862*
Finish: *Coast at Redwick ST 416 834* | **Maps:** *Ordnance Survey Landranger 171 Cardiff & Newport or OS Explorer 152 Newport & Pontypool*

Outline: Beyond Newport it's flat walking across fields and beside the narrowing mouth of the River Severn.

After following the bank of the Usk downstream from the Transporter Bridge, the path briefly skirts the vestiges of Newport's industry before heading across the fields to the Newport Wetlands RSPB Reserve. Winding past reedbeds, the way then follows the coast before turning in across a patchwork of meadows to Goldcliff. There's a bus there, but for accommodation you'll have to carry on, leaving the coast some 4 miles/6.4 kilometres further on to head inland to Redwick. **Note:** At Newport Wetlands, dogs are permitted on Rights of Way but not on other paths within the reserve.

Services: *You will find accommodation, a full range of services and road and rail transport off the route at Newport. There are pubs at Nash and Goldcliff, a café at the Newport Wetlands RSPB Reserve and light refreshments in summer on the coast at Gold Cliff. Goldcliff is served by bus, but has no immediate accommodation. However, there is a pub and limited accommodation close to the route at Redwick (but no bus). Newport TIC 01633 842 962 | newport.tic@newport.gov.uk*

Don't miss: Caerleon Fort – life in 2nd-century Roman Britain | **Newport Wetlands RSPB Reserve** – a wildlife haven on the edge of the city | **Redwick Church and museum** – the oldest peal of bells in the country

▲ *The broad mouth of the River Usk*

Newport

The Usk debouches through a broad tract of marsh, which forced the Romans to establish their river crossing and associated town well inland at Caerleon. A thousand years later, large areas had been drained, enabling the Normans to settle downstream at what is now Newport. Their *motte* and *bailey* was superseded by a 14th-century stone castle beside the river, the surviving remnant of curtain wall and Watergate Tower creating an impressive sight from Town Bridge. Today's lowest crossing remains the Transporter Bridge, which was built in 1906.

Although prospering as a medieval fishing and trading port, Newport's wharves could not accommodate the large ships of the 19th-century iron and coal trades. Therefore, its docks grew at the river mouth while industry crowded the river banks.

Since 2002 Newport has been a city and, despite the demise of coal, its economy has developed a broad base. Redevelopment is ongoing and the Alexandra docks remain busy, while large areas of former industry and the old marshes abound in nature. The whole of the River Usk is a designated SSSI and is renowned as one of the best salmon and trout rivers of southern Britain.

The Transporter Bridge's gondola carries vehicles and foot passengers across the River Usk

The route: **Newport Transporter Bridge to Redwick**

1 The coast path leaves beside the bridge through a kissing gate on the road's southern flank to head downstream on an **embankment** above the river. Beyond playing fields, riverside industry is largely screened from view, but quirkily the path mounts a **ladder stile over a conveyor belt** bringing aggregate from vessels berthed at the adjacent jetty. Eventually emerging by a **brickyard**, carry on along a service road that winds between industrial compounds.

2 Just beyond a **railway bridge**, as the road swings left, leave ahead along a cyclepath signed to 'Chepstow'. The path soon leaves the industry behind for scrub wood and rough grassland. After ½ mile/800 metres, the track swings left beneath power cables. Turn off right on a well-used path to a **bridge**. Over a track and **second bridge**, keep forward across flower-rich wet meadows to another **bridge**, immediately left of an indented corner. Strike half-left across the next meadow and over yet **another bridge** to continue

River traffic: *A freighter moving up the River Usk past West Usk lighthouse*

by the right-hand hedge. Through the field corner, carry on with the hedge now on the left. Faced with two bridges in the next corner, choose that in front. Stay by the left hedge, walking ahead beyond its corner to a **further bridge**. Maintain the same line towards the distant spire of Nash church across two more fields. Emerging onto a track, go left to the bend of a lane. Cross the road to a bridge and gate into the field opposite and make for a stile at the far side behind the **Waterloo Inn**.

Hay meadows are an increasingly rare sight in Britain, and those here, on the **Great Traston Meadows Reserve** *surrounded by reens, are particularly rich in rarer plants. They are at their best in summer when the fields are a mass of colour. Amongst the wildflowers you might find are yellow rattle and southern marsh orchid. Look out too for the grass vetchling, which for much of the year is hardly distinguishable from grass, but in early summer produces a delicate crimson, pea-shaped flower. Such a profusion of flowers attracts abundant insects such as butterflies, dragonflies and bees, including one of the smallest and rarest species, the shrill carder bee. They have a distinctive orange tip to the abdomen and the queen bee particularly, is fast in flight producing a very high-pitched buzzing. Amongst the birds to be seen are Cetti's warbler and reed bunting. You might also spot a barn owl hunting for small voles and perhaps see a grass snake or even an otter hunting along the reens.*

Sea of reeds: *Roosting starlings, bearded tits and otters all thrive in the RSPB Reserve's reedbeds*

3 Unless you want refreshment, stay in the field, walking behind the pub to a bridge. Carry on by the winding reen to another bridge in the corner and then strike across the next pasture to a crossing in the distant far right corner. Walk forward to a **gated bridge** on the left, over which head away by the left boundary. After crossing **two bridges**, swing right beside a reen and keep going over **more bridges** until you emerge onto a track. Go left for 150 metres then leave through kissing gates on the right. A grass track winds away between the ditches to emerge beside the 👁 **Newport Wetlands RSPB Reserve**.

4 Turn right to the car park and go left around the perimeter to find a path signed off to Goldcliff by a larger-than-life **reed mace sculpture**. Follow it on to a junction and swing left at the fringe of wetland scrub and reed-filled ponds. Ignore paths leading off left into the reserve and keep ahead with the main track, eventually winding beneath power cables and reaching the coast.

5 To the left, the way continues along the sea defences, overlooking a fringe of **saltmarsh** grazing and mud exposed at low tide. Some ½ mile/800 metres on is the **East Usk Lighthouse**, which, unlike its counterpart across the reach, remains operational.

Carry on for another mile/1.6 kilometres, turning right after a sharp left bend to remain with the coast and eventually dropping behind the **sea wall** to another junction.

The Gwent Levels extend for some 23 miles along the coast between the rivers Ely and Wye. A vast expanse of low-lying ground, much of it below sea level but with occasional islands of higher ground, it has been designated a Landscape of Outstanding Historic Interest and includes many Sites of Special Scientific

East Usk Lighthouse

Erected in 1893, East Usk Lighthouse complemented the already existing western light to guide shipping into the mouth of the River Usk. It was the first Trinity House light to incorporate the Dalén Sun Valve, a device that automatically switched on and ignited the gas supply as darkness fell. The light operated unmanned for a full year on 12 cylinders of gas. It was converted to electricity in 1972.

Saltmarsh and artificial scrapes at Newport Wetlands RSPB Reserve

Newport Wetlands RSPB Reserve

From ash tip to nature reserve

Extending over some 437 hectares, the reserve was established in 2000 by the RSPB in partnership with Natural Resources Wales and Newport City Council to mitigate the loss of wetlands caused by the creation of Cardiff Bay. Although it includes some farmland reclaimed from the Caldicote Levels, much of the site was once a fuel ash tip associated with the nearby power station. Within the reserve are a complex of reens, saline lagoons, reedbeds and wet grasslands, with saltmarsh and mudflats occupying the intertidal zone beside the Usk estuary. Located near the entrance to the reserve is an informative visitor centre and café.

There's usually plenty to see at any time of year, although autumn

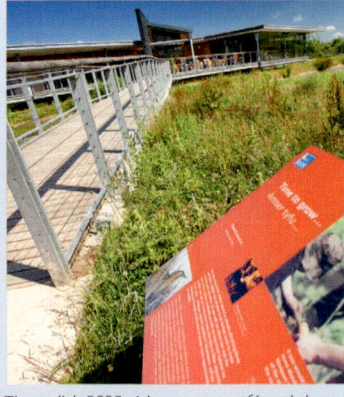

The stylish RSPB visitor centre, café and shop

and winter are sometimes considered the 'best' times for estuarine marshes. Migrating birds heading for Africa such as wheatear, redstart and willow warbler might pause to refuel, while others like ruff, dunlin, curlew and oystercatcher come to spend winter feeding on the marshes and mud flats. A spectacular sight is that of starlings, which often gather at dusk in murmurations or flocks numbering 60,000 or more. When the conditions are right they take to the sky in seemingly orchestrated displays in which the whole flock twist and weave in a beautiful aerial ballet, the air noisy with their chatter. Then, just as dramatically, they can disappear as they settle en-masse into the reeds to roost for the night.

Spring heralds the breeding season, with males singing to establish territories or entice a mate. As the year segues into summer, there is a frenzy of feeding and the young birds take to the air, building stamina for the long journey south.

Bad weather can throw migrating birds from their path and occasional rarities such as Savi's warbler, golden oriole and American widgeon have been spotted. The reserve also attracts predators and winter high tides are often a good time to look for short-eared owls when prey on the saltmarsh becomes more concentrated as it retreats before the advancing waterline. Over the course of a year, 150 different species of birds have been logged.

Migration signpost on the RSPB Reserve

"The Gwent Levels is the most important lowland wetland landscape in Wales"

The Wildlife Trusts

But there's more to see than just birds. Wildflowers include several orchids, flag iris, celery-leaved buttercups and rootless duckweed, the world's smallest flowering plant. You may also spot frogs, lizards and newts as well as adders and grass snakes. Small mammals include shrews, voles, stoats an weasels and perhaps even an otter, if you are lucky.

More information: For details, see: www.rspb.org.uk/Newport_Wetlands; phone 01633 636363

Neither land nor sea: *Tidal saltmarsh is a priceless but threatened natural habitat*

Interest. Surprisingly, today's landscape is completely man-made, for, until the Romans arrived, it consisted largely of fen and saltmarsh, regularly inundated by the Severn's massive tides. For prehistoric hunter-gatherers, it offered rich pickings of fish and wildfowl as well as game such as deer, boar and auroch. The silt and mud has preserved many archaeological traces and campsites, trackways and even human footprints have been discovered.

It was the Romans who first took up the challenge of changing the landscape by building protective banks along the coast below Caerleon to reclaim fertile land for pasture and arable farming. In addition to keeping the sea at bay, a network of drainage channels and ditches was necessary. Locally these are known as vurrows, ridges and reens, distinguishing the different functions they perform in draining rainwater from the fields and conducting streams to the sea.

Remains of a Roman sea wall have been found near the mouth of the River Rhymney and a settlement nearby perhaps oversaw grazing for cavalry horses, suggested by the large number of equine bones unearthed. Further along the coast, a Roman boundary stone was discovered by the mouth of Goldcliff Pill. However, after the Romans withdrew from Britain, the defences were largely abandoned and gradually breached, the land once more being inundated by the sea.

After the establishment of Norman rule, work began on repairing and extend-

ing the sea walls and drainage channels, often following the old Roman line. Many areas were reclaimed under monastic supervision; Tintern Abbey held large tracts of land as did Goldcliff Priory, first founded in 1133. These medieval reclamations can still be discerned in today's landscape and are characterised by land split between communal open fields and smaller, irregular enclosures surrounded by ditches that often followed the wandering course of existing streams. Scattered farmsteads, often incorporating orchards grew up, which were connected by a network of wide droves to allow movement of livestock between seasonal pastures. The back fen, that furthest from the sea and often lowest lying was more difficult to drain and generally left as common summer grazing.

The 14th century brought two setbacks; a small climate change led to more ferocious storms and in 1349 the Black Death swept across the country, decimating the population. Without the manpower to repair the damage, flooding returned and there was a managed retreat to maintain a more sustainable line further back from the sea. Tragedy struck again in the 17th century, when a disastrous flood overwhelmed the whole coast, claiming the lives of many.

Maintenance of the system of sea walls and reens requires the co-operative effort of landowners, farmers and villagers. Although Commissioners of Sewers had been established in the 15th century, there was no power of enforcement until the Caldicote and Wentlooge Levels Drainage Board was established in 1884. Under this, significantly more land was won, including parts of the back fen. These later reclamations can be distinguished by the geometric pattern of reens and tracks and are contemporary with the railway, which strikes arrow straight across the back fen.

Reclaimed farmland is protected by a carefully maintained sea wall

6 Although a path continues along the sea wall, the **official route** diverts inland to avoid disturbing sensitive bird sites. Bear left (not hard left), the way soon becoming tree-lined beside a reen. Emerging beside a cottage at **Saltmarsh Farm**, follow the ongoing lane for ½ mile/800 metres. Approaching sheds, leave through a signed gate on the right.

Follow the left boundary around to a **footbridge** and walk left to a **second bridge**. Over that, swing right, passing through a gate in the next corner to put the hedge back on your left. Across a wide gap behind a **farm**, keep going by the left edge of two more fields, crossing a **final bridge** onto a grass track. To the left it leads out to a road.

While industry has encroached onto the levels around Newport and Cardiff, much of the coastal strip remains under agriculture. The Newport Wetlands RSPB Reserve and Parc Tredelerch have been reclaimed from industrial wasteland, and the reens that divide and drain the land are important refuges for plants and wildlife. But preservation of the various habitats requires constant management; repairing sea walls, clearing ditches, servicing gouts (the simple flap valves through which water flows to the sea at low tide), reducing winter water levels to prevent flooding and raising them in summer for irrigation and ensuring water for livestock and wildlife.

In winter, the fields attract wildfowl and ducks while in spring you'll see breeding lapwing. The reed beds, hedges and pollarded willows provide both food and cover and attract many small birds such as warblers and buntings, while in the reens themselves you'll find amphibians, water beetles and water voles. The

Wild and free?: *Huge numbers of sandpipers and other waders overwinter on the Severn Estuary*

diversity of the salt marsh beyond the sea wall was once maintained by summer grazing, but although the practice has largely died out the foreshore remains a valuable feeding ground for birds. Indeed, it is reckoned that over 90,000 waders and wildfowl descend on this part of the Severn Estuary each winter.

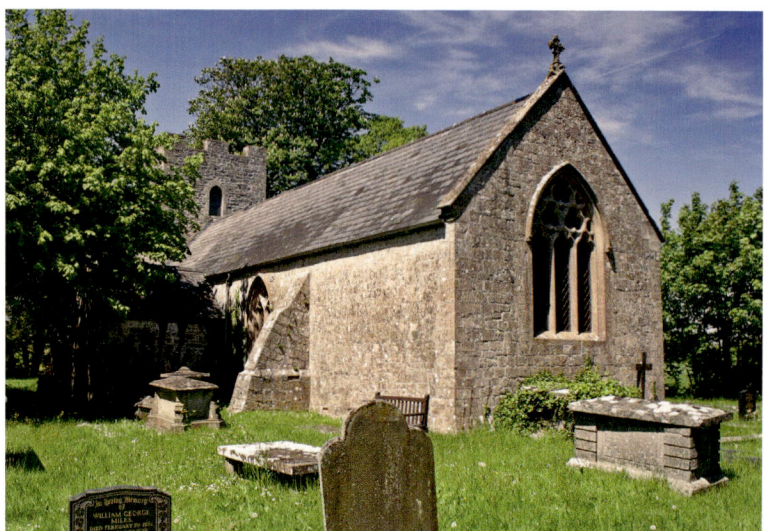

Historic tsunami?: *Inside Goldcliff church is a plaque commemorating the 'Great Flood' of 1607*

7 Walk right for 200 metres before turning off right along a metalled drive, which, beyond a gate, degrades to a hedged track. Approaching the coast, swing left with the embankment beside **Goldcliff Pill**, shortly returning to the lane in the village. The **Farmer's Arms** pub is just a short distance to the left.

If the church in Goldcliff is open, pop in and look towards the far end of the north wall for a memorial plaque that remembers 22 souls lost during the 'Great Flood' that occurred on the 20 January 1606 (or 30 January 1607 under the modern Gregorian calendar). A catastrophic tidal surge swept into the narrowing Bristol Channel, overwhelming the South Wales coast from Laugharne on the Taf estuary in Carmarthenshire up to Chepstow. The water flooded inland for up to two miles, destroying 26 villages and devastating the levels. The speed of the advancing water was so great that it overtook those attempting to flee and more than 3,000 people were drowned. The cause of the disaster remains uncertain, but it was probably a tsunami, originating from an undersea earthquake south of Ireland.

8 The onward route, however, lies to the right above the head of the pill. After 300 metres, turn off along a gravel track on the right. Through a gate, follow a grass swathe below an embankment, on top of which a couple of **birdwatching hides** gaze out across Goldcliff Pill. At the end of the swathe, bear left through a gate and walk on by the right ditch. Swing left within the corner, passing through to a second pasture and carrying on to a lane. Go right to the coast at **Gold Cliff**, where refreshments and snacks can be had most of the year from the **Sea Wall Tearooms**.

When Benedictine monks founded a priory here in 1113, Gold Cliff was an island cliff of limestone and mica that reflected the sun. It was the monks who resumed the work of pushing back the tide begun by the Romans. Giraldus Cambrensis noted when he passed by 70 years later, that 'the stone shines very bright and takes on a golden sheen' and conjectured that it might contain sweet honey and oil, a fitting place for the priory.

9 Climbing up steps onto the **embankment**, turn left as the route continues east beside the steadily narrowing estuary of the **River Severn**, passing **Porton House** and later a **pipeline** from the Llanwern Steelworks. Carry on for another 1¼ miles/2 kilometres to find, just beyond a **breakwater**, a track leading inland to Redwick.

Approaching Porton Grounds at low tide, look for lines of tall wooden staves stretching out from the bank. They are the remains of 'Putcher ranks', a traditional method of catching salmon. Large, cone-shaped baskets made of hazel and withy were fixed along the rank facing either up or down river, to trap salmon as they attempted to swim by on the tide. As the tide ebbed, the fishermen would go out to gather the catch, packing the fish in ice for transport to market. For a time, there was also a smokery at Porton where the salmon could be smoked. During the season, the fishermen slept in the fish house, for with the constant progression of the tides, it was a round-the-clock job. The practice was undertaken at several other places on both banks of the Severn Estuary, and may have been started by the monasteries or perhaps even pre-date Roman times.

10 Called **Sea Street Lane**, the track leads to **Redwick** ½ mile/800 metres inland, where there is accommodation at **Brick House**. **11** In the village, don't miss the unusual 👁 **Redwick church**, opposite the Rose Inn.

Lines of stakes in the mud are the remains of ancient fish traps

SECTION NINE

Redwick to Chepstow

Distance: *14¼ miles/23 kilometres* | **Start:** *Coast at Redwick ST 416 834* **Finish:** *Chepstow River Wye Bridge ST 536 942* | **Maps:** *Ordnance Survey Landranger 171 Cardiff & Newport and 162 Gloucester & Forest of Dean or OS Explorers 152 Newport & Pontypool and 154 Bristol West and OL14 Wye Valley & Forest of Dean*

Outline: The final leg is undemanding walking and follows the narrowing mouth of the River Severn past its lowest bridging point to Chepstow

The route continues at the edge of the saltmarsh, best experienced at low tide when waders come to feed. Further on, the official route diverts inland across Rogiet Moor to avoid a military firing range, returning to continue beside the river and pass beneath the impressive Second Severn Crossing viaduct. There's more engineering interest at Sudbrook, which stands above the Severn Tunnel before a final marsh nudges the path inland to Mathern. The last couple of miles turn above the River Wye, eventually leading to the town bridge in Chepstow and the end of your journey.

Services: *There are rail and bus links at Severn Junction and a bus service to Sudbrook. There are a few pubs, cafes and other services just inland at Caldicot, Portskewett and the St Pierre hotel. Chepstow is served by both rail and bus and has a full range of accommodation, shops, eateries and pubs, banks, post offices and other services. Chepstow TIC 01291 623772 | chepstow.tic@monmouthshire.gov.uk*

Don't miss: The Severn Bridges – Britain's longest bridges | Chepstow Castle – oldest medieval stone castle in the UK | Chepstow Museum – discover the history of Chepstow

▲ *Chepstow Castle on the River Wye*

Redwick

Although not strictly on the route, **Redwick** is just about the only place between Newport and Chepstow offering bed and breakfast.

The village dates from the Norman period, established amidst pastures claimed from the sea marsh. Indeed its name is said to mean 'dairy farm amongst the reeds'. Clustered around a meeting of roads by a church once held by Tintern Abbey, the farms were surrounded by orchards that supplied the area's once-important cider industry. Some of the old trees harbour clumps of mistletoe, a parasitic plant much loved for Christmas decorations. Beside the church is an odd building of modern construction, which serves as a small museum to house a number of old presses and examples of vernacular stonework.

The 12th century church is one of the largest in the area and is unusual in having a full immersion baptistry pool. Victorian glass in the east window is all that remains after the church was badly damaged by a stray bomb in August 1942. As you leave, look on the side of the porch for a mark showing the level to which the water rose during the Great Flood of 1607, while in the graveyard is the truncated shaft of a medieval preaching cross.

Redwick church and the unusual museum

The route: **Redwick to Chepstow**

1 If you've spent the night in **Redwick**, retrace your steps along **Sea Street Lane** back to the coast.

Ideas to build a barrage across the mouth of the Severn have been put forward since the middle of the 19th century, to carry road and rail links and create a vast shipping basin accessed by locks. That it could also incorporate turbines to produce electricity was considered as early as 1921, but as yet there remain many economic, engineering, environmental and no doubt political difficulties to overcome. Various lines for possible structures have been proposed, ranging from between Cardiff and Weston to as far upstream as Oldbury Sands, each producing different anticipated benefits and costs. Undoubtedly, there is potential to make a significant contribution to the country's energy requirement as well as create new direct transport routes, but the impact on the environmental landscape would be profound.

2 The onward route lies to the left beside the **Severn Estuary** for the next 3¼ miles/5.5 kilometres, passing a wastewater treatment plant, a farm and the occasional pill or outflow draining the marsh behind.

© Crown copyright and/or database right. All rights reserved. Licence number 100047867

Bridge club?: *Curious sheep stare as the coast path approaches the Severn Bridge*

Drawing you on, the two motorway bridges striding across the Severn estuary ahead mark the approaching end of the Coast Path and, if you have completed the entire trek, your 1400-kilometre (870-mile) journey around the coast of Wales. Eventually, as the trees thicken below, look for a marker directing the **official route** off the embankment to a series of gates leading to a lane towards Rogiet.

Some 50 metres further along the embankment beside the path is a trig column oddity. Obviously placed before the embankment was constructed, the concrete column is now all but buried and barely protrudes above ground. Although sited just above the beach, the trig column is not the lowest in the country. That lies near the Little Ouse in Cambridgeshire and is actually one metre below sea level. The one here is recorded as being nine metres above sea level.

Alternative route: *Keeping to the coast*
A Right of Way does continue along the embankment, but the **official route** is diverted inland to avoid a military firing range and sensitive coastal wildlife areas. Red flags fly when the range is in use and you must wait until sentries advise that it is safe to continue.

3 Heading inland, the leafy track soon gives way to hedges. Turn left along the road, to cross a cattle grid and bridge over the **motorway**.

Modern marvel: *The Second Severn Crossing is a triumph of civil engineering*

The lane ahead continues over the **railway line** past **Severn Tunnel Junction Station** into **Llanfihangel** and **Rogiet**. There are no services there but you can catch a bus or train if need be.

4 Take the first right over the motorway bridge to follow a narrow lane for almost 1½ miles/2.5 kilometres towards Caldicott. On reaching the train station (where a bridge under the railway leads to Caldicot), turn right along the lane.

5 As the lane bends towards a bridge, leave through a kissing gate on the right. A path leads away across a field to a **footbridge spanning the motorway**. Drop beyond to the coast and bear left to resume your eastward trek, the path shortly winding beneath the 👁 **Prince of Wales Bridge**, which carries the M4 motorway.

Until 1876, the lowest bridged crossing of the River Severn was at Gloucester. The new bridge above Sharpness was a prodigious feat of Victorian engineering, over ¾ mile long and carrying the Severn and Wye Railway on 22 wrought iron spans 70 feet above the river. Built to bring coal from the Forest of Dean, it later served as an alternative to the main line when the rail tunnel was closed for maintenance. However, in 1960, two fuel barges collided with one of the piers in thick fog, bringing down two of the spans. Four months later the bridge was further damaged when hit by a tanker, driven upstream by the tide after it had capsized off Beachley Point. As main line traffic was already being run through the Severn Tunnel, it was decided to dismantle what remained of the bridge.

Thomas Telford had proposed a road bridge across the Severn near Chepstow as long ago as 1824, but it was not until 1966 that the concept was realised when the first of the two motorway bridges was opened. Crossing both the Severn and

Sudbrook Iron Age fort

Like medieval Sudbrook village, much of the nearby Iron Age fort has been washed away by the river. Yet what remains of the embankment is an impressive feature, enclosing a large area now used as a playing field. It is thought to have been a base for the native Silures for about 200 years before the arrival of the Romans, who occupied it to oversee a ferry linking South Wales to the Roman settlement at Bath.

the Wye, it is almost a mile long and carries the M48 between England and Wales. Incorporating two lanes of traffic as well as pedestrian and cycle tracks in each direction, it replaced a ferry that operated between Beachley and Aust and which closed shortly after the motorway bridge became operational.

Thirty years later, the Second Severn Crossing (now named the Prince of Wales Bridge) was opened to accommodate ever-increasing volumes of traffic. Roughly following the line of the Severn Tunnel, it carries the M4 between Caldicot and Redwick and is over three miles long. Although providing three lanes in each direction, it lacks a pedestrian or cycle path.

6 Once under the bridge, go right through a gate and carry on along the embankment. Pass a recent housing development (on a former paper mill site), and go through a gate. Turn right over the undulating ramparts of **Sudbrook Iron Age fort**, a vantage later used for a **Second World War gun emplacement**, and follow the shoreline across the enclosure. At the far side, wind out past the **site of an old chapel** to a narrow lane and onto a street. Ahead is the **Severn Tunnel Museum**, open most days, and with toilets. Run by volunteers, it welcomes passing donations for its upkeep. The **Portskewett Inn** lies some ¾ mile/1 kilometre to the left, but the official route is to the right, over a disused rail track, and right again along the main street.

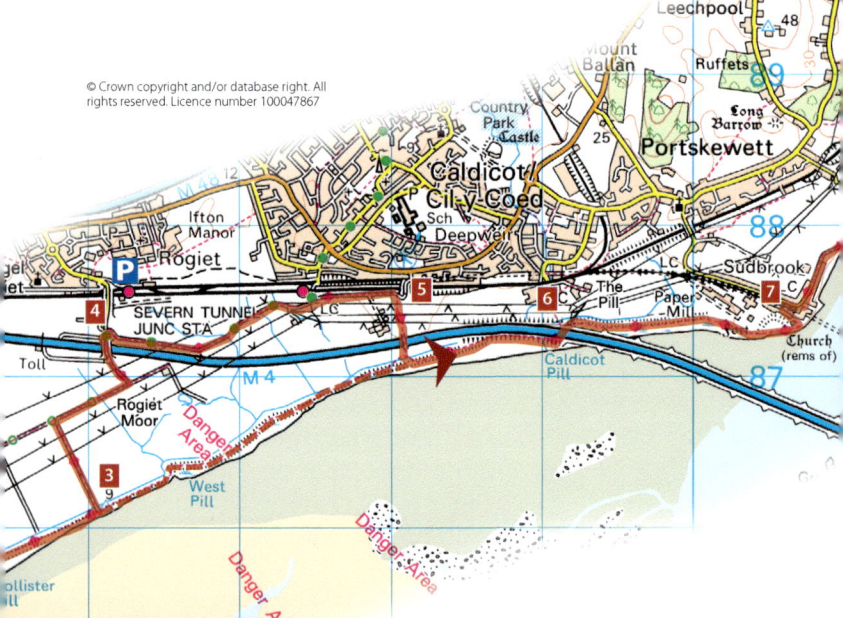

© Crown copyright and/or database right. All rights reserved. Licence number 100047867

Rock and stroll: *Crumbling sandstone cliffs line the river near Black Rock picnic area*

Opened in 1866, the rail tunnel took 13 years to complete and, at around 4½ miles, remained the longest such tunnel in Britain until HS1 began operating in 2007. An earlier attempt to push a tunnel beneath the river in 1810 failed when the river broke through and although flooding occurred again during construction of this tunnel, it was found to be spring rather than river water. The problem was eventually managed by channelling the water to the lowest point of the tunnel beneath Sudbrook and pumping it to the surface. The massive pumping station was originally powered by six steam engines and additionally serves to force fresh air through the tunnel.

The ruin of a 12th-century church is about all that remains of Sudbrook's medieval settlement, a victim of coastal erosion during the 14th and 15th centuries. The 'modern' village grew up to house workers employed digging the tunnel and included a school and infirmary. Many of the men were subsequently taken on in a shipbuilding enterprise, begun by the tunnel contractor and which remained in business until 1926. A later enterprise was a paper mill, which used the spring water pumped from the tunnel. It operated for almost fifty years before closing in 2006.

7 Follow the main street past the **Sudbrook Pumping Station**. Keep ahead past the last of the houses and a substation along a path that within ¼ mile/700 metres bears right to rejoins the coast at the **Black Rock picnic**

Wooden warrior: *A carved wooden sculpture of King Tewdric outside the church at Mathern*

area. Beyond, drop beside an **old jetty** and through a kissing gate to follow the beachhead below **low, crumbling cliffs** before rejoining the seawall to continue eastwards.

Alternative route: *Inland high tide route*

High tide floods the shore route, in which case, instead of dropping to the beachhead, follow a path left. Beyond the **car park** and a converted barn, take a track off right. Continue across a meadow to rejoin the coast through a kissing gate.

8 Approaching **St Pierre Pill**, back on the **official route**, drop from the embankment and follow a path beside a drainage ditch towards the railway. Through a gate, cross the level crossing, and walk on beside the lefthand reen. Beyond a second kissing gate, as the drain bends left, keep ahead to another kissing gate and continue straight across the next field. Keep going by the lefthand fence to a bridge, then bear half right to an indented corner by **Pill House**.

Bear right past the house and along the field edge to find a kissing gate and stone bridge, then left over a second bridge onto a **golf course**. Walk around a green to another bridge and maintain the same diagonal line across a large field. Through a gate in the corner, carry on along a track leading to a small

Section 9: **Redwick to Chepstow** 199

pump house. Turn right onto a lane running beside **St Tewdric's Church** into **Mathern**.

A successful 6th-century Celtic warrior king, Tewdric retired to a life of prayer at Tintern, but when the Saxons arrived, he returned to defend his people against the heathen in-

© Crown copyright and/or database right. All rights reserved. Licence number 100047867

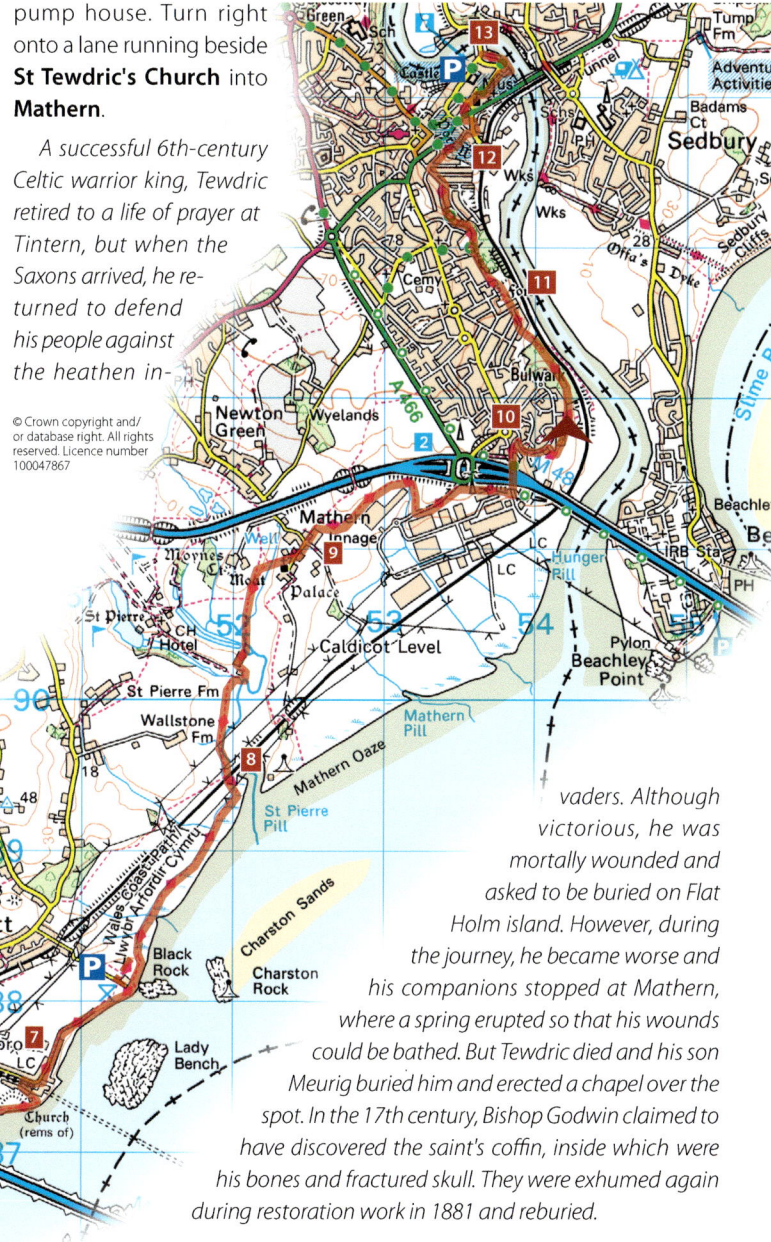

vaders. Although victorious, he was mortally wounded and asked to be buried on Flat Holm island. However, during the journey, he became worse and his companions stopped at Mathern, where a spring erupted so that his wounds could be bathed. But Tewdric died and his son Meurig buried him and erected a chapel over the spot. In the 17th century, Bishop Godwin claimed to have discovered the saint's coffin, inside which were his bones and fractured skull. They were exhumed again during restoration work in 1881 and reburied.

Border crossing: *The current Grade I listed Old Wye Bridge was constructed of cast iron in 1816*

9 Joining the main lane, walk forward to a junction by **Innage Farm** and pass through a kissing gate beside the entrance. Head on to a stile part-way along the right hedge. Over that, strike half-left to a gate in the far corner and carry on beside the boundary to leave by a stile in the corner.

A pleasant path winds on around a light industrial site, curving below the **motorway** to meet a service road. Cross to the continuing path opposite, which swings left as a **cycleway**. Keep left at a junction and then, meeting a broader track, go left beneath a **subway**, where a brightly painted mural welcomes you to **Chepstow**

10 Emerging beyond, follow the street ahead into a residential estate. At the end, turn right to the top of the hill and go right again into **Tenby Lane**. Approaching the end, beyond a residents' parking area, swing left beside a playing field and then behind houses. The path curves into trees, through which there is a view to the Severn Bridge across the mouth of the River Wye. Keep left with the main path past the rear of more houses and on along a linear **woodland trail**. Reaching a junction, walk right then fork left, descending steeply into the trees. *At the bottom, it is worth briefly diverting right, beneath the railway bridge, for a view of the river.* Return to the main path to continue past a small pumping station. Climb on beside the **railway embankment** then left back to the edge of housing.

11 Coming out on a street corner, go right on **Raglan Way**. Swing left at the end along **Victoria Road** but leave after 30 metres on a track between houses on the right. Keep ahead, passing the end of a street by the **Bulwark Camp** and on past a small industrial site back into trees.

Now just an open space, it was the site of a first-century BC Iron Age fort. The natural defences of a cliff and ravine were supplemented by a double-banked ditch, inside which archaeologists found traces of buildings from the Roman period.

Remaining with the higher path along the top fringe of the wood, keep ahead past a junction before gradually descending around the valley to emerge onto the end of a street. Follow it down to the end and turn left along **Hardwick Avenue**. At the top, keep right with the main street, but as it later sweeps left, walk ahead on a path that leads through a gap in the 13th-century **Port Wall**.

12 Follow the ongoing street down to the bottom of **School Hill**. Turn right in front of the post office along **Station Road** then go left past Tesco. Reaching the main road, cross using the subway just to the left. Climbing out on the far side, walk right along **Nelson Street** past a car park to **St Mary's Priory Church**. Bear off right along a railed path through the **churchyard** to emerge on **Lower Church Street** and then keep ahead past a Baptist chapel.

Where the street bends at the bottom, go right in front of the **Faraday Building** to the river front. Turn left along the old **quayside** past the **Boat Inn** and into a small park by the old bridge. There, you will find **standing stones** and a **roundel** set into the ground, which mark the end of the Wales Coast Path and the beginning of the Offa's Dyke Path. Chepstow's **ancient bridge** across the **River Wye**, which straddles the boundary between Wales and England lies just a few metres further on at **13**.

Now landscaped, the old waterfront is is an attractive setting to celebrate the **end of the walk** and your journey along the wonderful **Wales Coast Path**.

Useful Information

Wales Coast Path
Comprehensive information about all sections of the Wales Coast Path can be found at: www.walescoastpath.gov.uk and www.walescoastpath.co.uk

'Visit Wales'
The Visit Wales website covers everything from accommodation to attractions. For information on the area covered by this book see **www.visitwales.com/explore/west-wales** and www.visitwales.com/explore/south-wales

South Wales
For local information, from what to do to eating out, see www.southwalesattractions.co.uk. To find out about the Glamorgan Heritage Coast see **www.visitwales.com/destinations/south-wales/glamorgan-heritage-coast** and for the Newport Wetlands RSPB Reserve, go to **www.rspb.org.uk/reserves-and-events/reserves-a-z/newport-wetlands/**

Tourist Information Centres
The main TICs along the South Wales Coast provide free information on everything from accommodation and travel to what's on and walking advice.

Swansea	01792 468 321	tourism@swansea.gov.uk
Porthcawl	01656 786 639	porthcawltic@bridgend.gov.uk
Bridgend	01656 815 906	tourism@bridgend.gov.uk
Cardiff	029 2046 3833	visitor@cardiff.gov.uk
Newport	01633 842 962	newport.tic@newport.gov.uk
Chepstow	01291 623 772	chepstow.tic@monmouthshire.gov.uk

Where to stay
Accommodation ranges from hotels and guest-houses to holiday cottages and campsites. However, outside the cities and large towns, accommodation can sometimes be thin on the ground, but the position is constantly changing as new premises open to take advantage of gaps in the market. It is therefore wise to plan ahead and the several Tourist Information Centres in the area are a useful source of information and can sometimes even make a booking for you.

Walking holidays
Several companies offer complete walking packages including : accommodation, local information, maps, baggage transfer and transport.

Celtic Trails 01291 689774 | **www.celtictrailswalkingholidays.co.uk**
info@celtic-trails.com

Train and buses
For public transport information across Wales, see **Traveline Cymru** 0871 200 22 33 | www.traveline.cymru. The main towns and cities are served by rail and bus services run within the conurbations, as well as radiating to many of the smaller villages.

Taxis
Numerous taxi firms operate within and around South Wales towns and cities.

Cycle hire & repair
There are cycle hire and repair shops in the main towns and cities along the way.
Swansea – **The Bike Hub**, 78 St Helens Road SA1 4BQ | 01792 466944 | www.swanseabikeshop.blogspot.co.uk; Port Talbot – **Welsh Coast Cycles**, 1 Cambrian Place SA13 1HD | 01639 894169 | www.welshcoastcycles.co.uk; Porthcawl – **Onit Cycles**, 4 Eastern Promenade CF36 5TS | 01656 857202 | www.onitsports.co.uk; Cardiff – **Cyclopaedia**, 116 Crwys Rd, CF24 4NR | 029 2037 7772 | www.cyclopaedia.co.uk; Newport - **South Wales Bicycle Co**, 45 Caerleon Road NP19 7BW | 01633 243384 | www.southwalesbikes.co.uk.

Boat Trips
Boat trips are available around Cardiff Bay or further afield to Flat Holm in the middle of the Bristol Channel. Check out www.bayislandvoyages.co.uk or www.cardiffcruises.co.uk

Emergencies
In an emergency, call 999 or 112 and ask for the emergency service you require: Coast Guard, Ambulance, Police or Fire. For non-emergency or general enquiries to South Wales Police call 01656 655 555 or 101.

Tides
Short stretches of the Wales Coast Path and alternative routes are only accessible on a low or outgoing tide. Check tide times before you go. Tide table booklets are widely available from TICs and local shops for around £1. For today's local tide information for places along the South Wales Coast see: www.tidetimes.org.uk

Weather forecasts
For reliable, up-to-date weather forecasts, see www.bbc.co.uk/weather or www.metoffice.gov.uk/public/weather/forecast

Access to large scale Ordnance Survey mapping

A major new feature of the website offers access to **large scale Ordnance Survey mapping** showing the route for each official Day Section. This can be used on a smart phone, along with the locator feature, to find and follow the users position at any point on the path.

Accommodation booking

A new accommodation booking feature has been added to the website enabling quick, easy booking for a range of accommodation at the beginning and end of each official Day Section, on any of the seven sections of the Wales Coast Path.

In addition, you will be able to book a range of local day trips, transport options—including national and international flights, and vehicle hire.

Wales Coast Path: Official Guides

The **Official Guides** to the **Wales Coast Path** are endorsed by Natural Resources Wales, the Welsh government body which developed and manage the path. The guides break the Wales Coast Path into seven main sections, giving long-distance and local walkers everything they need to enjoy all 870 miles of this world-class route.

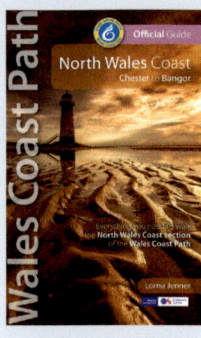

North Wales Coast
Chester to Bangor
ISBN: 978-1-914589-00-3

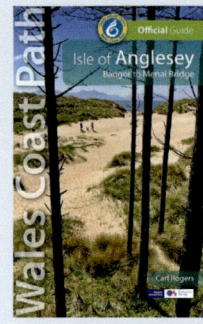

Isle of Anglesey
Circuit from Menai Bridge
ISBN: 978-1-914589-01-0

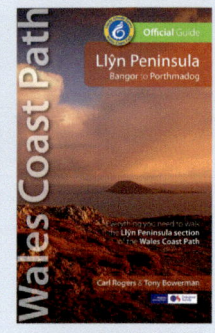

Llŷn Peninsula
Bangor to Porthmadog
ISBN: 978-1-914589-02-7

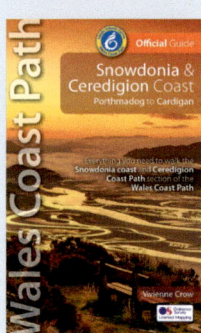

Snowdonia & Ceredigion Coast
Porthmadog to Cardigan
ISBN: 978-1-914589-03-4

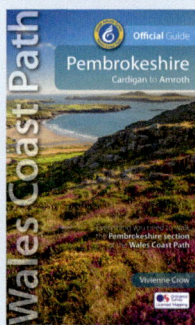

Pembrokeshire
Cardigan to Amroth
ISBN: 978-1-908632-98-2

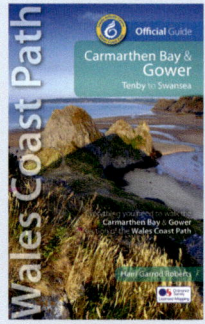

Carmarthenshire & Gower
Tenby to Swansea
ISBN: 978-1-908632-99-9

Wales Coast Path: Top 10 Walks

Award-winning pocket-size walking guides to the most popular, easy circular walks along key sections of the Wales Coast Path. The full series will cover the whole path in ten attractive guides.

Buy online at: www.northerneyebooks.co.uk

Currently available

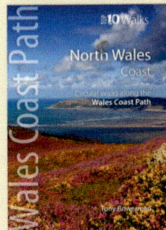

**Top 10 Walks:
North Wales Coast**
ISBN: 978-1-908632-15-9

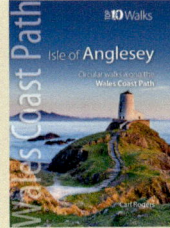

**Top 10 Walks:
Isle of Anglesey**
ISBN: 978-1 902512-31-0

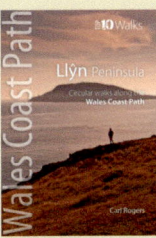

**Top 10 Walks:
Llyn Peninsula**
ISBN: 978-1-902512-34-1

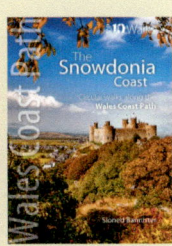

**Top 10 Walks:
Snowdonia Coast**
ISBN: 978-1 908632-85-2

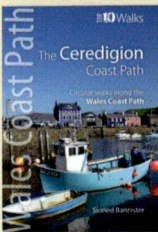

**Top 10 Walks:
The Ceredigion Coast**
ISBN: 978-1-908632-28-9

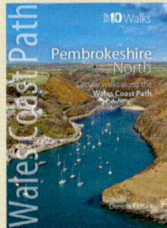

**Top 10 Walks:
Pembrokeshire North**
ISBN: 978-1-908632-29-6

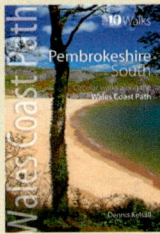

**Top 10 Walks:
Pembrokeshire South**
ISBN: 978-1 908632-30-2

**Top 10 Walks:
Carmarthenshire & Gower**
ISBN: 978-1-908632-16-6

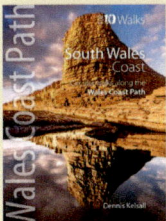

**Top 10 Walks:
South Wales Coast**
ISBN: 978-1-908632-31-9

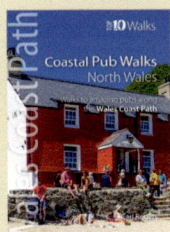

**Top 10 Walks:
Coastal Pub Walks
North Wales**
ISBN: 978-1 908632-82-1

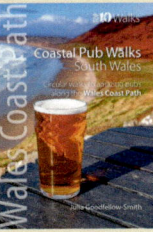

**Top 10 Walks: Coastal
Pub Walks
South Wales**
ISBN: 978-1-914589-15-7

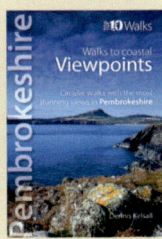

**Top 10 Walks: Walks to
Coatal Viewpoints
Pembrokeshire**
ISBN: 978-1-908632-93-7